KU-485-053

SOUTH ASIAN
POLITICAL SYSTEMS

General Editor
RICHARD L. PARK

The Politics of Nepal

PERSISTENCE AND CHANGE
IN AN ASIAN MONARCHY

LEO E. ROSE *and*
MARGARET W. FISHER

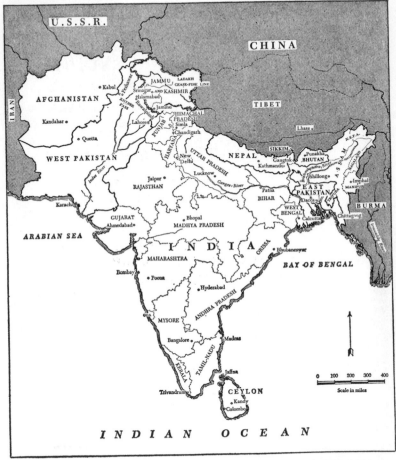

U.S.S.R.

CHINA

IRAN

AFGHANISTAN

Kabul

Peshawar

KHYBER
PASS

Rawalpindi

Islamabad

JAMMU
AND KASHMIR

LADAKH
CEASE-FIRE LINE

Srinagar

Jammu

HIMACHAL
PRADESH

Simla

PUNJAB

Chandigarh

HARYANA

Lahore

New
Delhi

UTTAR PRADESH

Lucknow

NEPAL

Kathmandu

TIBET

Lhasa

SIKKIM

Gangtok

BHUTAN

Punakha

Shillong

A S S A M

N.E.F.A.

NAGALAND

Kandahar

Quetta

WEST PAKISTAN

Indus River

Karachi

Jaipur

RAJASTHAN

Ganges River

Patna

BIHAR

Brahmaputra River

EAST
PAKISTAN

Dacca

WEST
BENGAL

Calcutta

Chittagong

MANIPUR

Imphal

BURMA

Irrawaddy River

GUJARAT

Ahmedabad

Bhopal

MADHYA PRADESH

I N D I A

ORISSA

Bhubaneswar

BAY OF BENGAL

ARABIAN SEA

MAHARASHTRA

Bombay

Poona

Hyderabad

ANDHRA PRADESH

GOA

MYSORE

Bangalore

Madras

KERALA

TAMIL-NADU

Jaffna

Trivandrum

CEYLON

Kandy

Colombo

0 100 200 300 400

Scale in miles

I N D I A N   O C E A N

SOUTH ASIA

TELEPEN

6 00 131004 4

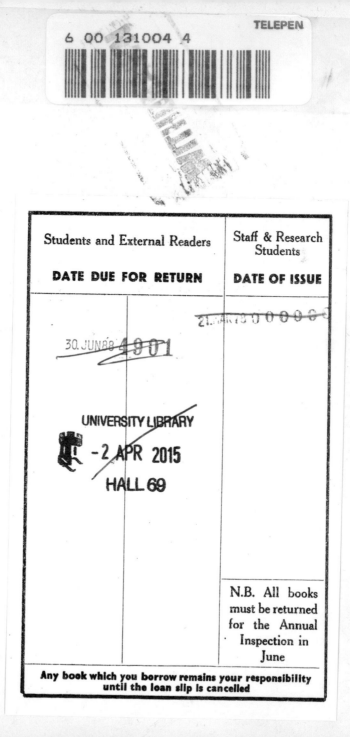

Students and External Readers	Staff & Research Students
DATE DUE FOR RETURN	**DATE OF ISSUE**
30. JUN88 4901	21.
UNIVERSITY LIBRARY -2 APR 2015 HALL 69	
	N.B. All books must be returned for the Annual Inspection in June

Any book which you borrow remains your responsibility
until the loan slip is cancelled

The Politics of Nepal

PERSISTENCE AND CHANGE
IN AN ASIAN MONARCHY

LEO E. ROSE *and*
MARGARET W. FISHER

UNIVERSITY LIBRARY
NOTTINGHAM

Cornell University Press

ITHACA AND LONDON

Copyright © 1970 by Cornell University

All rights reserved. Except for brief quotations in a review, this book, or parts thereof, must not be reproduced
in any form without permission in writing from the pub-
lisher. For information address Cornell University Press,
124 Roberts Place, Ithaca, New York 14850.

First published 1970

International Standard Book Number 0-8014-0574-2
Library of Congress Catalog Card Number 72-120291

PRINTED IN THE UNITED STATES OF AMERICA
BY VAIL-BALLOU PRESS, INC.

To Our Nepali Friends
and Colleagues

Foreword

Serious study of modern South Asia is a relatively recent development in the United States. It began shortly after World War II, and was made possible by opportunities for language study and research in the region. Scholarly work on current South Asian themes, however, rests upon older academic traditions that emphasized principally the philosophy, religion, and classical literature of these ancient civilizations. This series, "South Asian Political Systems," is addressed to contemporary political problems, but is presented in the context of institutions and value systems that were centuries in the making.

Over the past quarter century, humanists and social scientists in Asia, Europe, the United States, and elsewhere throughout the world have worked together to study modern South Asian cultures. Their efforts have been encouraged by a recognition of the importance of the rapid rise of nationalism in Asia in the twentieth century, by the decline, hastened by the war, of Western imperial systems, and by the appearance of dozens of independent states since the founding of the United Nations. Scholars were made increasingly aware that the South Asian peoples were not anonymous masses or abstract representatives of distant traditions. They were, like us, concerned with their own political affairs, with raising families, building houses, constructing industries, educating the young, and creating better societies. They were nourished by their heritage, but they also struggled to devise political institutions, economic processes, and social organizations that were responsive to modern needs. And their needs were, and continue to be, great.

It was an awareness of these realities that encouraged private foundations and agencies of government to sponsor intensive field work in South Asia, including firsthand observation of day-to-day life and opportunities to discover and use rare source material. India has received the most attention, in part because of its size and intrinsic importance, in part because scholars have concentrated on teaching Indian languages, and research tends to be done where the languages are understood. More and more the other countries of South Asia—Pakistan, Nepal, Ceylon, and Afghanistan—have begun to attract scholarly attention. Whereas in the late 1940's one was hard pressed to find literature about the region, except in journalistic accounts or in British imperial histories, by the 1970's competent monographs and reliable periodicals are abundantly available. Today one can draw from an impressive bibliography on South Asia, including a commendable list of political works.

It remains true, however, that recent South Asian studies have been largely monographic—books that examine narrow themes in detail and that appeal to a small group of specialists who happen to be concerned with these themes. There are few broad guides to the politics of the countries of South Asia. This series has been designed to fill part of the need.

One of the problems in writing introductory works is that learning about a foreign culture is never a simple process. Experience tells us that each political system is imbedded in a broader social system, which in turn has roots in a particular history and a unique set of values. Language transmits culture, so one way to approach an unfamiliar culture is through the close study of language and literature. Knowledge of history, or of the arts, or of social organization offers another path to understanding.

The focus of this series is on political systems. Each author starts with a common organizational framework— brief history, political dynamics, political structure, continuing problems—and weaves in unique factors. For India, a complex federal organization of government and a varied and changing political party system require emphasis. For Pakistan, the constitutional dilemma is the most crucial issue. For Nepal and Afghanistan, monarchical traditions in conflict with pressures to modernize necessitate treatments that are more historically oriented. Ceylon, too, has political problems, especially ethnic and religious, not readily comparable with others. Used together the books should provide excellent opportunities for comparison and contrast.

This volume on Nepal is the work of Margaret W. Fisher and Leo E. Rose, of the University of California, Berkeley, distinguished students of the Himalayan region. Their earlier work on India led them to examine the northern reaches of Nepal, Ladakh, Sikkim, Bhutan, and the tribal areas of Assam. Nepal, a country long neglected by scholars, has received in their hands the scrupulous care that it deserves. They have labored devotedly to convey that which took them many years to comprehend; they have contributed a useful, readily understandable, and systematic introduction to the Nepalese political system.

RICHARD L. PARK

Ann Arbor, Michigan
June 1970

Preface

Our collaboration in researches on Nepal began in 1952 and has continued, with varying degrees of intensity, down to the present. In the early fifties, Nepal was emerging from centuries of seclusion, but was still largely unknown to the outside world. In the course of its search for a place in the modern world a palace revolution occurred which toppled a singularly anachronistic system of government. For a brief period Nepal won attention—although something less than comprehension—in the world press.

Our search for answers to questions arising from journalistic accounts of these events proved to be more rewarding than we had expected. Initial curiosity gave way to sustained interest in the unique civilization which had developed in Nepal's mountain fastnesses. It became clear that this civilization, the people who had created it, and the environment which had nurtured it offered a variety of challenging problems worthy of the attention of scholars in all fields.

To the political scientist, Nepal is of special interest, partly because it is an Asian country that was never reduced to colonial status. Its traditional institutions, well established and widely accepted, are today undergoing change, but the change is being initiated and controlled by Nepalis unconditioned by Western conquest. Nepal is also one of the few countries in Asia where the modernizing of the traditional institutional structure is occurring with a monarchy as the chief agency of change. (Iran and Afghanistan also come to mind, but neither is as clear an example as Nepal.) Inherent in this situation is the persistence of a traditional approach to politics which conditions the direction and pace of change, sometimes introducing unexpected complications. Old ways of doing things are frequently given new names and new ways are given old names, so that it is sometimes difficult to discern which developments represent persistence and which represent change. Whether this approach has been applied intuitively or as a conscious exercise of statecraft must for the present remain unanswered. Of greater importance is the degree of success which has thus far attended its use.

Nepal's efforts to maintain its national identity, given its geopolitical situation, have prompted it to develop both an internal polity and a foreign policy that distinguish it from its two powerful neighbors, India and China. This distinction has been achieved internally through the panchayat system, and externally through an extension of the nonalignment concept to the goal of "equal friendship for all."

The process of change continues apace. Indeed, Nepal's overall stability appears to be enhanced by, if not actually dependent upon, fairly constant change. In any event, we are discussing a country that is still in transition. Today's analysis will not necessarily provide a prognosis for tomorrow's developments, but hopefully it will aid in making them comprehensible.

It is a pleasure to acknowledge indebtedness to the following: Richard L. Park, the general editor of this series, at whose invitation this particular work was undertaken; the Institute of International Studies, University of California, Berkeley, for support of our researches; the American Institute of Indian Studies, for support in 1963–1964; officers of His Majesty's Government, for many courtesies; friends in Nepal and India who contributed in various ways, and particularly Rishikesh Shaha, Mahesh C. Regmi, Surya Prasad Upadhyaya, Pasupati Shamsher, D. R. Regmi, General Mrigendra Rana, Major-General Subarna Shamsher, Dr. Satish Kumar, Dr. B. P. Poudel, and Purna Bahadur, M.A.; colleagues at the University of California, with special mention for Robert A. Scalapino and Joan V. Bondurant; colleagues connected with the Himalayan Border Countries Project, and above all Bhuwanlal Joshi, John T. Hitchcock, Frederick H. Gaige, Jagdish Sharma, Kunjar Mani Sharma, and Roger Dial; and, finally, Cleo C. Stoker, Senior Administrative Assistant at the Institute of International Studies, for the many ways in which she facilitated the work.

We of course give to one and all the customary absolution and take upon ourselves full responsibility for any errors of fact or interpretation.

LEO E. ROSE
MARGARET W. FISHER

Berkeley, California
June 1970

Contents

Foreword, by Richard L. Park   vii

Preface   xi

1. Political and Social Heritage   1
2. The Monarchy and Representative Institutions   34
3. The Administrative and Judicial Systems   63
4. Political Forces in Nepal   92
5. The Modernization of the Nepali Economy   120
6. Nepal's International Relations   144
7. Modernizing Nepali Politics   164

A Guide to the Literature on Nepal   177

Suggestions for Further Reading   193

Index   195

Maps

South Asia   *Frontispiece*

Nepal   *Page 3*

The Politics of Nepal

PERSISTENCE AND CHANGE
IN AN ASIAN MONARCHY

1. Political and Social Heritage

The Hindu kingdom of Nepal occupies a central position on the southern slopes of the great 1,500-mile Himalayan mountain system which separates the Tibetan plateau from the plains of the Indian subcontinent. Nepal's capital city, Kathmandu, lies sheltered in a verdant intermontane valley within a setting no less magnificent than that of the larger and more celebrated Vale of Kashmir.

The early history of the valley, known simply as Nepal (or Nepal Valley) in the country, but now generally called Kathmandu Valley by foreigners, reaches back into legendary times. When and by whom the valley was first settled is not known. There is, however, fragmentary evidence to show that flourishing communities existed there as early as the sixth century B.C. Dynastic chronicles bear testimony to the continuing prosperity of the valley over the centuries, but no clear picture of the history of this period emerges. It is a reasonable presumption however, that until about the seventh century cultural influences reaching the valley from the outside world came mainly from the south, and were therefore Indian in origin.

In the early years of the seventh century (or perhaps even a few years before), the situation appears to have abruptly changed; Tibetans suddenly put in an appearance in the valley, having made their way over the Kerong Pass.[1] Tibet at this time was swiftly rising to a position of military dominance in central Asia. Indeed, the Tibetan monarch was strong enough to demand, and receive, both a Nepali princess and a Chinese princess in marriage. A new capital was also established at Lhasa, making feasible a more direct route between India and China by way of Kathmandu Valley. For several decades this route eclipsed the long-established but more roundabout access through Kashmir Valley. The new route was eventually closed between Lhasa and the Chinese capital because of the intermittent warfare characterizing Tibet's relations with China, and several centuries elapsed before the route could regain its original importance. Nevertheless, the opening of the Kerong Pass radically changed Kathmandu Valley from a remote corner to a strategic way station, allowing it to exercise a high degree of control over traffic between the markets of India and those beyond the high Himalayas. This position has vitally affected Nepal's subsequent history down to the present day. A distinctive civilization evolved in the valley, molded in part by the interplay of diverse cultural and intellectual influences originating beyond its borders, but bearing above all the unique impress of the gifted and vigorous Nepali people. The impetus toward creating a synthesis of basically discordant elements has remained strong in Nepal, but the task has become more difficult. Now that hostility between its powerful neighbors seems to have become chronic,

---

[1] Baburam Acharya, "Anshu Verma Ra Unaka Rajyakal Ko Rajniti Tatha Sanskriti" [Anshuvarma and Affairs Related to the Politics and Culture of His Time], *Jhankar* (Nepali weekly), Year 2, Issue 7, Baisakh 2018 (March–April, 1961), p. 5.

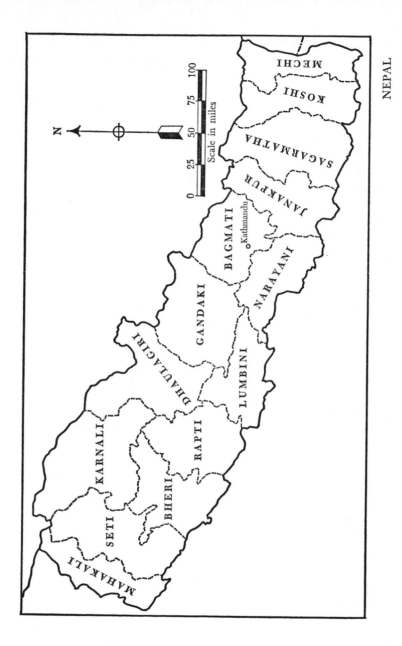

NEPAL

Nepal has found its established way of life subjected to severe and irreconcilable ideological and political presures.[2]

The Geographic Setting

With Tibet under Chinese military occupation, geopolitical considerations involving Nepal have indeed grown in importance. But Nepal's dramatic geography has in fact always strongly conditioned its history. Certain salient geographic features must be recognized for adequate comprehension of Nepal, whether the focus be on history, internal politics, foreign policy, or developmental problems.

Nepal is a relatively small country, about the size of Illinois. Nevertheless, its approximately 670-mile northern border with Tibet constitutes nearly one-third of the total Himalayan bastion upon which the Indian subcontinent has long relied for protection. Included in Nepal's portion of the border are fourteen passes in general use, several of which are of considerable strategic importance. One of these is the Kuti–Kodari Pass which has now been connected with both Kathmandu and Lhasa (and hence to Peking) by Chinese-built roads—the first all-weather motorable highway to breach the main Himalayan axis.

On Nepal's eastern border lies the tiny Indian protectorate of Sikkim. The border here consists of the rugged bulk of Kangchenjunga (28,146 feet) and the Singalila Ridge. South of the Sikkim line, the hills constituting Nepal's eastern border with Darjeeling District in West Ben-

2 Nepal is described in the 1962 Constitution as a "Hindu monarchy," and in this respect it has taken a more extreme position than India, which despite its preponderant Hindu majority proclaims itself to be a "secular state."

gal are far less formidable. Furthermore, India's narrow corridor into Assam, which runs between East Pakistan on the south and Sikkim and Bhutan on the north, verges on the southeast corner of Nepal. At this point, Nepal and East Pakistan are separated by no more than about twenty miles of Indian territory.

Nepal's western border is the Kali River, but the Kali drains only a narrow strip of westernmost Nepal. To the west lies the Kumaun Himalaya, in the Indian state of Uttar Pradesh. With the exception of this western fringe (and of the bowl-like Kathmandu Valley, whose rivers rise within the rim of the bowl and exit from it through a single gorge), most of Nepal can be described as the drainage basin of three mighty river systems. From west to east these systems are generally known as the Karnali, the Gandak, and the Koshi. Each of these great river systems includes one or more tributaries which rise in Tibet and enter Nepal through deep gorges. Each system also has tributaries of glacial origin which must descend some 20,000 feet before reaching the Nepali plains. Floods and landslides are the natural consequence. All of Nepal's rivers eventually reach the Ganges. Since Nepal's share of the Gangetic plain is a very narrow belt along the Indian border—averaging about ten miles in width and seldom, if ever, exceeding twenty—the floods which so frequently devastate communications in Nepal also bring disaster to India. Thus a number of considerations, arising from Nepal's geography, tend to involve the two countries in each other's destinies.

Nepal's major river systems with their deep gorges and rugged transverse ridges have greatly hindered the development of east–west communications. In the past, travelers wishing to reach points in eastern or western Nepal from Kathmandu ordinarily followed a circuitous route—descending to India, crossing the plains to an appropriate point for re-entry into Nepal, and then traveling northwards. The administrative and political unification of the country has always been hampered by these difficulties. The present government, despite the almost prohibitive costs of construction and maintenance, places great emphasis on an east–west highway to provide easier access to outer areas of the country.

A traveler wishing to cross Nepal from the Indian plains north to the Tibetan plateau might have to pass through, in a mere hundred air miles, as many as eight distinct zones: the Terai, the Siwalik mountain zone, the Inner Terai, the Mahabharat Range, the midlands, the Himalayan Range, the high mountain valleys of the Inner Himalaya, and finally the border mountains.[3]

The southernmost strip of Nepali territory, known as the Terai, was once mostly a dense jungle, highly esteemed for big-game hunting in the cold season, but shunned during the rest of the year because of the prevalence of a virulent form of malaria. In an earlier period this malarial belt was considered to be an important asset in the defense of Kathmandu. It was only in the latter part of the nineteenth century, after relations between Nepal and British India had improved, that efforts were made to clear this area for cultivation. Today the region yields about three-fourths of Nepal's total revenue. For-

---

[3] This classification follows that of the Swiss geologist Toni Hagen, who carried out a seven-year geological survey of the entire country. See his *Nepal: The Kingdom in the Himalayas,* tr. by Britta M. Charleston (Berne, Switzerland: Kummerly and Frey, 1961).

ested areas still abound in the Terai, but there are now several roads across this belt which connect the Indian plains with points in the Nepali hills. One such road is the Indian-built highway (the Tribhuvan Rajpath) to Kathmandu.

The Siwalik mountain chain is of the sharp, "hog-back" type. On the average it rises only 4,500 feet above sea level, and its highest summits lie below 6,000 feet. There are few settlements in the Siwalik zone because of lack of water in the dry season.

Between the Siwalik and Mahabharat ranges in central Nepal are several long narrow valleys called Vitri Madhesh or the Inner Terai. The soil here is very fertile and water is plentiful but the prevalence of malaria has long discouraged the clearing of this area for cultivation. Two of these valleys—Rapti and Hetaunda—have recently been made suitable for habitation, and prospects for further development are encouraging.

The Mahabharat Range, with peaks attaining an elevation of nearly 10,000 feet, is considerably higher than the Siwalik chain and is Nepal's principal defensive wall on the south. It is cut by a few deep gorges through which the great river systems flow, but these gorges are so wild that, from the point of view of defense, they are of less consequence than the higher passes eroded by the monsoon rains. The range is too steep to be densely populated, but small settlements (*garhis*) dot the hills where trade routes cross the range. These *garhis* (established originally for defense purposes) serve as customs posts and check points between the major divisions of Nepal—its Terai and "hill" regions.

The midland region lying between the Mahabharat and

Himalayan ranges is the most heavily populated part of Nepal. High transverse ridges separate the great river systems, and a ring of mountains encircles Kathmandu Valley, but most of this midland region lies between 2,000 and 6,000 feet. The area is further segmented into natural subdivisions by broad rivers. Major streams form junctions in this region before finally breaching the Mahabharat Range.

The Himalayan Range towers over the midlands, rising with breath-taking abruptness. The gorges which cut this range are some of the deepest to be found anywhere in the world. Settlements climb up these giant mountains to about 12,000 feet. Above this level is a belt of dense forest which gives way to alpine pasture which, in turn, extends to the snow line. High above, often veiled by clouds, tower the Himalayan snow peaks, including the world's highest (Mount Everest, or Sagarmatha as it is known locally), the only mountain whose summit is more than 29,000 feet above sea level. Nepal can lay claim to more "Eight Thousanders" (mountains in excess of 8,000 meters) than any other country in the world.

Some of the high peaks are on the boundary line, but others are well to the south. North of the crestline, but still within Nepal, lies a series of ten wide mountain valleys known as the Inner Himalaya. One of these valleys was caused by a transverse rift, but the others resulted from river erosion and run roughly parallel to the crestline. In elevation these valleys range from about 8,000 to nearly 20,000 feet. Secluded villages are to be found there.

The final zone is the range which marks the southern margin of the Tibetan plateau. The peaks here are somewhat less lofty than those of the Himalayan crestline, but form the principal watershed between the Ganges and Tibetan waters.

Ethnic Composition

Nepal's population (expected to surpass eleven million in the 1971 census) is nearly as diverse as its terrain. Indeed, to a large extent the population in the rural area tends to group itself ethnically according to elevation—which is to say by type of agriculture, as conditioned by elevation.

The territory now known as Nepal has offered shelter to waves of migrants for at least two millennia, and in all probability for much longer. The process has not yet come to an end. Within historic times migrants have entered Nepal to escape from enemies or to seek economic betterment, and earlier migrations probably had similar motivations.

Migration traditions have often become encrusted with mythological lore or lost altogether. Nevertheless, we know that certain ancestors of the present population moved into Nepal from the southeast as part of a vast movement of peoples from southeast Asia and the southern borders of China. Some, whatever circuitous routes they may have traveled, had their homeland in regions north of Nepal. Others moved northward from the Indian plains, and yet others migrated eastward after a generation or more in the Kumaun Hills.

It can be said that the dominant strains in the population are Caucasoid and Mongoloid, with varying degrees of admixture; but to be more explicit would be difficult. No meaningful figures for the size of the different ethnic groups as they now exist can be given since this category is not employed in the official census.[4] Many groups have been reduced to scattered remnants about which little or nothing is known. Even with the larger groups, systematic ethnological study is in its infancy. Several different attempts have been made to classify Nepal's ethnic groups, but no two classifications are in agreement, and they often differ sharply in important particulars. It is clear that efforts in this field have been premature, and we shall confine our discussion to brief comments on the better-known groups.

The dominant group socially and politically is made up of the descendants of high-caste Hindus from India who took refuge in Nepal centuries ago. Some are now concentrated in Kathmandu, but others of this group have kept their rural ties and are to be found scattered throughout the midlands, rarely settling above 6,000 feet. They form the local elite wherever they reside, and have long dominated politics at the central level. Their language is Nepali and their religion is Hinduism. Their main subdivisions are Brahmans and Kshatriyas. The most important Kshatriya subdivisions are the Thakuri, to which the royal house belongs, and a group with numerous subdivisions, known collectively as Chettri. The most important of these subdivisions are the Ranas, who governed Nepal for a century as hereditary prime ministers until the prerogatives of the royal house were restored in 1951.

[4] Figures are given for the number of speakers of various languages, but these cannot safely be equated with ethnic origin, as persons able to speak Nepali would normally be so enumerated without mention of their mother tongue. The size of an ethnic group would accordingly be underestimated, and the error would be magnified in terms of percentages of the population as a whole.

Beginning with the latter part of the nineteenth century, migrants of a different class were allowed to enter Nepal from the Indian plains. They are largely farmers and laborers, although there are merchants and Brahmans among them. They have played a major role in the development of the Terai. Both Hindus and Muslims are represented in this migration. In appearance, language, and culture, they are indistinguishable from their Indian neighbors on the other side of the border.

Among the oldest inhabitants of the Terai are the Tharus, a tribal group whose habitat extends in both directions across the Indo-Nepalese border. The Tharus are described as a "mixed" tribe, with no agreement as to their fundamental ethnic affiliation.

Another and far more important group, whose ethnic affiliations are also subject to controversy, is the Newari population centered in Kathmandu Valley. The Newars are characteristically an urban group—the builders of the distinctive civilization which has been developed in the valley. Their literacy rate is high, and they are heavily represented in the bureaucracy. The skilled artisans of Nepal are Newars. The bulk of the country's commerce is conducted by Newars. Their language, sometimes called Newari and sometimes Nepal bhasha ("the speech of Nepal" [Valley]), is fundamentally different from Nepali, but has so far eluded precise classification. Included among the Newars are both Hindu and Buddhist subgroups, although Hinduism has won a dominant position. Many who remain within the Buddhist fold have adopted certain Hindu rituals and social practices.

The remaining ethnic groups of numerical importance are unquestionably Mongoloid. They are sometimes classed together as "Tibeto-Nepalese" (as distinguished from "Indo-Nepalese"), but the term "Tibeto-Nepalese" is better reserved for the relatively recent migrants known to have come from Tibet, with "paleo-Mongoloid" used as a generic term for tribal groups of unknown antecedents long resident in Nepal.

Prominent among the paleo-Mongoloids resident mainly in the midland area west of Nepal Valley are the Magars and Gurungs—the tribes most favored by the British for the recruitment of the famed "Gurkha" soldiers. East of the valley are to be found the Rais and Limbus, sometimes classed together as Kiratis. Their ancient customs have been less affected by Hinduism than have those of the Magars or even the Gurungs, and regional sentiment is stronger. The Limbus, for example, are making a serious effort to revive their local language as a literary medium after long years of its suppression under Gorkha rule. Demands for broad regional autonomy continue to be voiced by some elements among these groups, in contrast to the growth of the trend toward nation-building observable in most regions of Nepal.

In the hills north of and adjoining Kathmandu Valley are the Tamangs, whose aboriginal tribal culture has been influenced by Buddhism but scarcely at all by Hinduism. The Tamangs, because of the poor quality of their land holdings, have been forced to support themselves as tenant farmers, day laborers, and porters.

The relatively recent migrants from Tibet have prospered in their new environment. Among these groups are the Sherpas, who have in recent decades won international fame for their personal qualities as well as for their capacity to endure strain at high elevation—so vital to the success of Himalayan mountaineering. Sherpa prosperity, however, was founded originally on trade between Nepal and Tibet; they plied the passes in eastern Nepal. In religion they are Buddhist, and their language and culture unmistakably proclaim their Tibetan origin.

The counterparts of the Sherpas in western Nepal are the Thakalis, whose prosperity has also been based on the Tibetan trade. Just as the Magars, and to a lesser extent the Gurungs, have been more affected by Hinduism than the tribal groups in the eastern midlands, so too the Thakalis have been more affected than the Sherpas. Leading commercial families among the Thakalis have adopted certain Hindu customs, and their family priests are Brahmans. The future of the Thakalis, as of the Sherpas (and other smaller groups of Tibetan origin, usually known simply as Bhotes, or Tibetans) has been adversely affected not only by the constriction of trade since the 1959 revolt in Tibet, but also by the refusal of Chinese authorities in Tibet to permit the customary seasonal movement of livestock across the border. This has annulled grazing rights going back at least two centuries which had previously provided the basis for extensive sheep and yak herding.

The research required before the full complexity of Nepal's ethnic structure can be set forth has only just begun. Much also remains to be discovered concerning Nepal's equally complex social and cultural systems. But it is already evident that Nepal's cultural pattern can be distinguished in significant respects from that of India. Indeed, Nepali nationalism stresses those aspects of the Nepali ethos which are distinct from that of India. The line of demarcation is often imprecise, however, as it is also evident that cultural influences from India—whether emanating from Hinduism, Buddhism, or contemporary political ideology have had a decisive role in shaping many aspects of Nepali society. The acculturation process, in operation at the dawn of recorded history, was accelerated by the large-scale migration of high-caste Hindus to Nepal, especially during the twelfth to fifteenth centuries. The present dynasty, as well as the greater part of the local elite throughout the midmontane region, takes pride in its descent from these high-born refugees.

Hinduism, then, has for several hundred years been the official religion of the Nepali ruling class. Hindu social and ritual practices have carried the highest prestige value throughout most of the country. This does not mean, of course, that non-Hindus have always accepted the imposition of Brahmanic codes willingly, or that the mutual adaptation achieved between Buddhism and Hinduism was necessarily painless when first initiated. Nevertheless, despite occasional local opposition, the trend toward the adoption of Hindu ritual and social practices is probably more widespread today than in the past. And this widening of influence has been achieved despite the fact that the younger intellectuals, like their Indian counterparts before them, are beginning to reject certain traditional Hindu concepts and values which seem to conflict with their distinctly "modernist" orientation. Indeed, the most dynamic aspect of current social and cultural development in Nepal lies in this area of interaction between Brahmanizing and modernizing processes. The character of Nepali society in the near future will be largely determined by the nature of the mutual adjustment attained by these competing forces.

Modern History

The modern history of Nepal dates from that period in the latter half of the eighteenth century when the tiny principality of Gorkha, under the leadership of a king belonging to one branch of the Shah family, suddenly began to expand its domains. Before this expansion was checked, all of the sub-Himalayan hill areas between Bhutan in the east and the Sutlej River in the west had been brought under control. More than seventy-five small hill principalities submitted, either voluntarily or after unsuccessful resistance to the formidable Gorkha armies. By 1806, these armies were threatening to sweep on to Kashmir, but were turned back by the Sikh armies of Ranjit Singh.

The Gorkha drive to bring a 1,500-mile arc of Himalayan hill territory under one ruler was thus blunted, but the degree of success achieved by Gorkha arms was nevertheless remarkable. Not many years earlier, tiny Gorkha had been hard put to withstand the onslaughts of neighboring principalities of comparable size. What were the circumstances that enabled Gorkha to obtain dominion over a vast stretch of hill area so rapidly? One important factor was its strategic location with respect both to Kathmandu Valley and to the lucrative trade route between the valley and Tibet. Gorkha was well situated to take advantage of the political and economic crises which had become chronic in the wealthy but strife-ridden valley. The conquest of Nuwakot (on the trade route to Tibet) and Makwanpur (on the trade route to India) effectively isolated the valley and made possible its ultimate fall.

Gorkha's political leadership was also far more astute than that of most contiguous hill areas. King Prithvi Narayan Shah of Gorkha, heeding the lessons to be learned from the successes of Indian forces in the service of the East India Company, established the first modern regular army among the hill principalities. But of no less importance was the fact that Gorkha had developed the most comprehensive social and legal code in the hills, where there was a saying that "if one wanted justice, one should go to Gorkha." Without the attractions of Gorkha justice for the hill peoples and of trading opportunities for Newar merchants, the towns of Kathmandu Valley would not have fallen so readily to Prithvi Narayan. With Kathmandu in their possession (1769), the Gorkhalis were afforded both the financial resources to carry out further campaigns and the administrative facilities needed to retain their conquests.

In the process of empire-building, the new rulers of Nepal did make two serious miscalculations. The first was the attempt in 1791 to reduce Tibet to vassal status. Tibet called for Chinese help, and in the following year the Gorkhalis were surprised by a large army which had been assembled to drive them back across the Himalaya. The fighting in Nepal was inconclusive, but came to an end with the onset of winter. The Chinese and Tibetan commanders were anxious to remove their troops before snows closed the passes, and the Gorkhalis were equally anxious to make peace before the cold season would leave the malarial southern borderlands open to the passage of British troops. It became the fashion for historians to refer to the peace settlement which ended this war as "humiliating" to Nepal, but the Chinese as well as the Nepali official accounts make it clear that this is a misconception.[5] Through

5 *Ch'in-ting K'uo-erh-ka chi-lüeh;* compiled and printed, 1795, by order of the Emperor Ch'ien-lung, 32 books in 58 *chüans.*

this agreement Nepal was brought into a system of direct relationship with Peking which, in the crucial decades that followed, was of some importance in discouraging Nepal's absorption into the British Indian empire. But the war did not result in any great loss of territory, nor did it interfere with Nepal's campaign of expansion throughout the hills. Nepal was for the most part treated by China as an unruly and troublesome neighbor rather than as a vassal. The Nepalis, in their efforts to keep the British at arm's length, made much of their periodic "tribute" missions to Peking, but as was customary for missions from small states with whom the Ch'ing dynasty had diplomatic relations, the gifts the Nepalis received in exchange in Peking far outweighed in value those offered to the Chinese emperor.[6] Nepali missions, furthermore, frequently engaged in highly profitable (if illegal) opium trading on the side and were more than once denied access to China proper.

A more serious miscalculation was the decision in 1814 to contend with the British in India, who were determined to bring Gorkha expansion to an end. The Nepali army again conducted a remarkable struggle against considerable odds, making peace only when British forces had penetrated the outer defenses and were poised for the final march on Kathmandu. This defeat was more serious than any suffered in the war with China. Nepal lost Sikkim in the east, all of the hill areas beyond the Kali (the present boundary) in the west, and most of the revenue-rich plains area in the south (some parts of which were later

[6] The term used by Nepalis in describing the items presented to the Chinese emperor was *saugauli*, which should be translated as "gift" rather than "tribute." Furthermore, the same term was used for the presents received by the King of Nepal in exchange.

restored in recognition of Nepal's assistance to the British during the 1857 uprising in India). Nepal also obtained a more accurate appreciation of the depth of British power. Subsequent Nepali governments maintained an interest in anti-British alliances, but any direct confrontation with British India was thereafter sedulously avoided.

It is a remarkable commentary on Gorkha's dynamic qualities that the period of its most vigorous expansion was also characterized by chronic internal strife within its ruling elite, serious enough to threaten periodically to tear apart the newly established empire. The strongly centralized authority that successive Shah monarchs had won for their dynasty in Gorkha did not long survive the transfer of the capital to Kathmandu in 1770 and the death of Prithvi Narayan Shah in 1775. By the end of the eighteenth century, the political position of the ruling family had been thoroughly undermined and a number of Kshatriya (military caste) families were contending for power. It was a disaster for the Shahs that the throne, except for a brief, chaotic interlude in the last decade of the eighteenth century, was occupied by minors from 1777 to 1832. Regents and ministers (*mukhtiyars*) were thus able to concentrate authority in their own hands, virtually isolating the king from the political process.

Furthermore, Gorkha's rapid expansion had brought a number of influential high-caste families with no established tradition of loyalty or service to the Shah dynasty within the scope of Gorkha rule. The Kathmandu court found it expedient, indeed necessary, to absorb these families, which were usually well entrenched in local areas, into the central political system. In the process, the existing division of functions and offices at the court among

Gorkha-based noble families was disrupted, and a new equilibrium had to be achieved. This process of adjustment and accommodation occurred while the throne was easy prey to encroachment upon its rights and privileges, and the courtier families were quick to enhance their own position and prestige at the expense of the royal powers.

The political system in this period, thus, was characterized by a highly segmented, pyramidal structure dominated by a handful of Kshatriya families, assisted and advised by a number of prominent Brahman families. The allocation of power and influence among and within these families shifted from time to time: the Chautarias (a collateral branch of the Shah family) were dominant from 1785 to 1794; the Pande family, from 1799 to 1804; and the Thapas, from 1806 to 1837. Nevertheless, the patterns, goals, and methods of the political process remained substantially unchanged. All these families operated the administration in essentially the same fashion, their overriding consideration being the enhancement of their own material and political fortunes. The familial system thus provided the core of the political system, and primary loyalty was to family rather than to nation or monarchy. The administration was likewise staffed along familial lines, and army commands were divided among the elite families or various branches of a dominant family. The number of regiments assigned to a family came to be the most reliable index to its relative power and influence.

The Shah dynasty during this period never completely lost its political prerogatives. Indeed, the Throne, as the ultimate source of the legitimization required by each succeeding government, continued to provide the only continuity and stability experienced in Nepal during the long years of complicated maneuvers and countermaneuvers by rival Kshatriya families. But the ruling family itself was not immune to political ambition and its behavior was often characterized by the same spirit of familial advancement that animated the nobility. This was most in evidence in the period between the fall of the Thapa family (1837) and the emergence of the Rana family (1846), when King Rajendra (the first of his line to reach his majority since Rana Bahadur Shah in 1792) made desperate efforts to revive the authority of the royal family. The basic political situation was unfavorable, however, and his efforts ultimately brought disaster to the royal dynasty.

THE RANA FAMILY REGIME

King Rajendra's attempts to play off contending political factions against one another led to political anarchy as ministry succeeded ministry in rapid succession. The country reached the verge of civil war and possible total disintegration. Adding to the seriousness of the situation was the fact that the British, their conquest of India complete, were not inclined to tolerate explosive instability on their flanks. That Nepal was once again spared the fate of other Hindu kingdoms in the subcontinent is attributable in part to the country's natural defenses, but in even larger measure to the emergence of another strong and brilliant political leader, Jang Bahadur Kunwar, better known to history as Jang Bahadur Rana.

This remarkable man was able to smash all rival political factions in an efficiently conducted massacre in the royal palace courtyard (1846), after which he stripped the king of political power and centralized absolute power in the hands of his own family. He introduced one innovation which distinguished the Rana regime from earlier family regimes. The position of his family within the political structure was institutionalized in the Sanad (royal decree) of 1856, extracted from the reluctant but helpless reigning monarch, King Surendra. This document, which provided the legal basis for the Rana regime, granted Jang Bahadur and his successors absolute authority in civil and military administration, justice, and foreign relations, including the right to ignore the commands of the king if these should be considered inappropriate or contrary to national interests. The royal family thus surrendered all of its sovereign powers, and henceforth was kept secluded in the palace grounds. In return, the Shah kings were styled by the more exalted, if somewhat ironic, title of "Maharajadhiraj" (King of Kings).

The 1856 Sanad also bestowed the title of Maharaja of Kaski and Lamjung (two minor principalities in the western hills near Gorkha) upon Jang Bahadur and his successors. The full political significance of this move remains unclear, as Jang Bahadur never gave any public indication as to his motives in wrenching this concession from King Surendra. It has been suggested that this was intended as a first step toward the eventual deposition of the Shah dynasty and his own elevation to the throne of Nepal. If so, he later abandoned this intention. In any event, the social status of the Kunwars—who had been granted the right to the distinguished title of "Rana"—was greatly enhanced. Their position was henceforth higher than the rest of the Nepali nobility and equivalent to that of the royal house when its rule was confined to Gorkha.

Even more significant, the Ranas could now aspire to marital alliances with the Shah dynasty of Nepal and with Rajput ruling families in India.

Since the 1856 Sanad also bestowed the office of prime minister upon the Ranas in perpetuity, the question arose of the system of succession within the family. To gain the support of his ambitious younger brothers, Jang Bahadur had earlier promised that each of them would succeed to the prime ministership in order of seniority. This promise was honored in the roll of succession to the prime ministership prepared by Jang Bahadur on which all eligible members of the Rana family were ranked by generation and date of birth.

More important from the political viewpoint was the question of the succession to the office of Maharaja of Kaski and Lamjung, as it was in this office that the 1856 Sanad had delegated absolute authority. The roll of succession had nothing to say upon this point, but from the terminology used in the 1856 Sanad it would appear that Jang Bahadur's intention was to establish primogeniture as the principle of succession in Kaski and Lamjung, according to the pattern followed by the Shah family for succession to the throne of Nepal. Jang Bahadur's eldest son would then have inherited the title of maharaja and the full powers attached thereto, and the office of prime minister (inherited by his brothers) would have been stripped of its extraordinary powers. But any plans Jang Bahadur may have conceived to protect the interests of his sons were thwarted by his brothers. In 1877 upon Jang Bahadur's death—which occurred under very suspicious circumstances—his two surviving brothers forced the King to appoint the elder, Ranuddip Singh, as both prime minister and Maharaja of Kaski and Lamjung, a precedent which was followed by all succeeding Rana prime ministers. Jang Bahadur's sons later questioned the legality of Ranuddip Singh's succession as Maharaja, but to no avail.

It became the practice for each succeeding prime minister to tamper with the roll of succession, using all means at his disposal to place his own brothers and sons higher up on the rolls by excluding or demoting members of other branches of the family. This was actually less a matter of favoritism than of survival, since under the Rana system no prime minister could hope to remain in power for long unless his immediate branch of the family held most of the key civil and military posts. One unfortunate result was that no established or respected procedures for placement and advancement on the rolls were evolved. The self-interest of each ruling prime minister could all too often thwart orderly succession.

Developments within the Rana family which served to divide it on caste as well as subbranch lines also seriously affected the succession system and, eventually, the regime itself. In 1856 only ritually pure members of the family— i.e., the sons of a Rana by a wife of equal caste status— were placed on the roll. Jang Bahadur himself later violated this principle, however, by adding two of his sons to the roll despite their impure caste. This precedent was followed by Bir Shamsher (1885–1901), who placed his impure caste half brothers and sons on the roll.

Prime Minister Chandra Shamsher (1901–1928), who had several sons by high-caste wives, undertook to reverse the trend of developments by dividing the Rana family into "A," "B," and "C" categories. The "A" Ranas were the progeny of wives with whom any high-caste Kshatriya could interdine freely according to orthodox caste principles; "B" Ranas were born of wives with whom all social intercourse except the partaking of boiled rice was permissible; and "C" Ranas were the children of consorts with whom orthodox Hindu marital ceremonies were barred. By this system, Chandra Shamsher sought to preserve the privileges of the highest-caste Ranas while at the same time formally associating "B" and "C" Ranas with the lower echelons of authority in the military and civil administration. For example, on reaching their majority, "A" Ranas were automatically given the rank of lieutenant colonel, while "C" Ranas became captains. The "B" and "C" Ranas, however, could rise only to the rank of colonel and major, respectively. This rule effectively barred them from succession to the prime ministership since this post could be attained only after advancing through the top military commands, including commander-in-chief.

Chandra's successor, Bhim Shamsher, who had several class "C" sons, ignored this regulation in drawing up a new roll of succession. With Bhim's death in 1932, the new Prime Minister, Juddha Shamsher, decided to reintroduce the caste principle into the succession system. In the wake of the disastrous earthquake of 1934, Juddha suddenly removed all "C" Ranas from the roll, appointing most of them to positions in the district administration where they would be comparatively harmless.

Juddha's policy, although successful in the short run, had serious long-term repercussions. The solidity of the Rana family, never very strong at best, was virtually destroyed by this ill-conceived action. A wealthy and powerful class of Ranas emerged with no real stake in the preservation of the family regime. A number of "C" Ranas, with extensive interests in Indian industrial and commercial enterprises, subsequently joined other Nepalis in a determined bid to destroy the regime. This breach in the Rana family structure contributed substantially to the overthrow of the regime in 1951, after 104 years of absolute authority in Nepal.

THE "DEMOCRATIZATION" OF NEPALI POLITICS

The period immediately following World War II brought a multitude of tribulations to the government of Nepal. The British withdrawal from India not only deprived the Ranas of powerful external backing, but placed in power in New Delhi a government whose attitude toward the Ranas was anything but sympathetic. The small but vocal group of anti-Rana Nepalis in India was for the first time given an opportunity to organize politically and to use India as a base from which to subvert the Nepali government. Internal discontent also began to assume dangerous proportions, not only in Kathmandu where it could be controlled, but also in the districts adjacent to India where Rana authority could be effectively challenged. Moreover, potential threats to the regime came from more than one direction. When the Communists came to power on the Chinese mainland in 1949, they immediately proclaimed their intention to "liberate" Tibet and re-establish China's "traditional" boundaries in the frontier region. While these "traditional" boundaries were not precisely defined, Nepal's supposed "vassalage" to the Ch'ing dynasty was referred to in ominous terms.

At the moment of its greatest crisis, the top echelon of the Rana family was too seriously divided on policy to be capable of decisive, purposeful action. Padma Shamsher, who had succeeded to the prime ministership in 1946, made several, largely ineffectual attempts to reduce the arbitrary character of the regime. A few reforms were introduced, including a new constitutional system that modified, without fundamentally altering, the Rana political structure, and for the first time the exercise of civil liberties on a limited scale was permitted. But the sons of Chandra Shamsher, who continued to hold most of the top posts under the new Prime Minister, were reluctant to accept even these modest reforms and were finally able to force Padma's resignation in April, 1948. His successor, Mohan Shamsher, immediately reversed the direction of state policy. Implementation of the new constitution, promulgated in January, 1948, was quietly postponed, and stern repressive measures to control the opposition were reintroduced. The effect, however, was not what had been intended. The position of the government continued to deteriorate, with the result that when Mohan Shamsher, in a desperate, last-ditch effort in 1950, decided to give effect to the 1948 Constitution, it was already too late.

The crisis for the Rana regime came in November, 1950, with a series of events both within and outside of Nepal. On November 6, King Tribhuvan sought and received asylum in the Indian Embassy. Four days later, he was flown to New Delhi in an Indian Air Force plane. The same day, anti-Rana forces in India, led by the recently formed Nepali Congress, launched a series of attacks across the border in the Nepal Terai. These events coincided closely with the Communist Chinese invasion of eastern Tibet which had commenced in October, 1950. Increasingly concerned with the trend of developments, the

Indian government decided to give qualified support to the King and the Nepali Congress by pressing the Ranas to accept a compromise settlement that would liberalize the regime and, hopefully, prevent Nepal from becoming prey to communist contagion from the north. New Delhi's preference was for a gradual transition during which "popular" forces would gain an expanding role in the administration, but, to assure stability, would initially be associated with the existing regime.

A cease-fire on these terms was eventually reached in New Delhi. On February 18, now celebrated as National Day, King Tribhuvan issued a royal proclamation which, in effect, terminated the Rana monopoly of political power but permitted Ranas to retain certain offices at his discretion. A coalition Rana-Nepali Congress cabinet was formed, with Mohan Shamsher as Prime Minister. The Nepali Congress Home Minister, B. P. Koirala, however, commanded majority support in the cabinet and possessed more real power.

A government composed of such incompatible elements had scant expectation of survival. The Nepali Congress ministers, suspecting Rana sabotage of their reform program, demanded the right to form a "homogeneous" cabinet. After a series of moves and countermoves in which the Ranas attempted to turn the tables on the Nepali Congress by organizing certain popular forces against B. P. Koirala, the King dismissed the ill-assorted cabinet on November 11, 1951, and appointed a new government composed entirely of Nepali Congressmen. Surprisingly, however, not B. P. Koirala, but his half brother, M. P. Koirala, was appointed Prime Minister.

The first of what was to become a series of experiments

with the form and structure of the government thus came to an end. The "homogeneous" one-party government proved to be no more successful, however, as the Nepali Congress was deeply split, both by personal rivalry between the Koirala brothers and by a fundamental lack of agreement within the party on basic political, economic, and social questions. The first M. P. Koirala government was forced to resign in August, 1952, when the Prime Minister and most of his cabinet colleagues were expelled from the Nepali Congress.

Unwilling to accept B. P. Koirala as Prime Minister, but unable to find a suitable alternative, King Tribhuvan finally decided to dispense with "popular" government for the time being and to rule directly through an advisory council, organized on cabinet lines and composed of non-party leaders. This was unpopular with virtually all organized political groups. The "independents"—mostly non-Ranas who had been closely connected with the Rana regime—were well pleased but in no position to offer the King effective support. In any case, it was obvious that King Tribhuvan, whose health was poor, viewed direct rule as a burdensome expedient to be terminated as soon as a party government to his taste could be formed. Finally, in August, 1953, he once again called upon M. P. Koirala to form a government based upon the newly established National Democratic Party.

The Prime Minister was instructed to work toward the formation of a coalition government in which all major political forces except the Ranas and the Communists would be represented. The result, whether intended or not, was a "national government" that excluded not only the Communists and Ranas, but also the Nepali Congress, still the only significant political organization in the country. The "national" character of the four-party coalition was thus seriously compromised, and the component parties, insignificant in themselves, soon fell to bickering with one another. It was a relief to the public and cabinet alike when M. P. Koirala's resignation was finally accepted in March, 1955.

King Tribhuvan's death in April, 1955, and the accession of Crown Prince Mahendra to the throne marked another turning point in the transitional politics of post-Rana Nepal. The new ruler quickly demonstrated his determination to participate directly and actively in the political process, a dramatic change from the passive role preferred by his father. King Mahendra immediately introduced a novel direct rule system in which he served as *de facto* prime minister as well as head of state. Meanwhile, negotiations between the various political parties were held under his direct supervision and upon his terms. Once it became evident that no acceptable coalition government could be formed, the King decided upon a one-party government based upon the Praja Parishad—a small party that had instigated an unsuccessful conspiracy against the Ranas in the late 1930's—buttressed by several "independents" with close ties to the Palace. Tanka Prasad Acharya, the head of the Praja Parishad, was asked to form a government in January, 1956.

The Praja Parishad cabinet, as reorganized a few months later, lasted for nearly eighteen months and had a number of accomplishments to its credit in such matters as land reform, administrative reorganization, and economic development through planning. But it made no impression on the basic political situation in which opposition forces, led by the Nepali Congress, were obviously gaining in strength. King Mahendra, in mid-1957, for reasons which never became clear, embarked upon a startling experiment. Tanka Prasad Acharya was replaced by the colorful K. I. Singh, who headed a small splinter party known as the United Democratic Party.[7] All other parties were united in their opposition to this move. The experiment did not last long. The King and his new Prime Minister fell out within three months, and K. I. Singh was summarily dismissed in November, 1957.

The King next considered a somewhat different system of direct rule—an experiment with "national" government in which he would himself function as Prime Minister in a cabinet composed of party leaders of his own selection. In his discussions with political leaders, the main points at issue were the character and composition of the cabinet. Most of the parties were prepared to accept the King as Prime Minister, although reluctantly, but opposed his plan for selecting which party leaders should serve in the cabinet, fearing this would give the King an unwarranted influence in party affairs.

At this time there was also a dispute between the King and several party leaders over the general elections scheduled for February, 1959. Most of the parties insisted that the body to be elected should be a constituent assembly, as King Tribhuvan had promised in 1951. King Mahendra,

---

[7] K. I. Singh, one of the Nepali Congress military commanders in the 1950 revolt, had refused to abide by the cease-fire agreement and had been imprisoned. After an abortive *coup d'état* attempt by his supporters in January, 1952, K. I. Singh escaped from prison and fled to Communist China. He returned to Nepal in the fall of 1955, and not long thereafter received a full pardon from King Mahendra.

on the other hand, wished to have the constitution prepared under his supervision and granted to the country
under his sovereign powers after which elections for a parliament would be held. The parties finally accepted the
King's proposals. A four-party "caretaker" advisory council was formed—composed of the Nepali Congress, Gorkha
Parishad, Nepali National Congress, and Praja Parishad
—to prepare the country for the elections.

All things considered, the general elections of 1959 were
conducted peacefully and with few serious malpractices.
Parliamentary democracy was launched under the most
auspicious circumstances possible. Even more surprising
were the election results. The Nepali Congress, which
most observers had expected to win a bare majority at
best, swept to an overwhelming victory, winning more
than two-thirds of the seats in the lower house. The result,
which seemed to presage the end of political instability,
was greeted with general satisfaction by the public. A
party cabinet whose right to govern was based upon a
solid majority in an elected legislature was now in office,
presumably until at least the next general election five
years hence.

The new government, headed by B. P. Koirala, demonstrated unprecedented vigor and determination in implementing the party's moderate democratic-socialist program. Conservative political and economic factions were
able to arouse some opposition to the government's policies and programs outside of Parliament, but were helpless in the face of the huge Nepali Congress majority in
the legislature. Indeed, King Mahendra's increasing dissatisfaction with the course of developments was the only serious threat to the cabinet. Particularly disturbing to the

King, reportedly, was the Ministry's handling of riots and disorders in the district of Gorkha, the homeland of the Shah dynasty. Perhaps even more crucial was his evident dissatisfaction with the pallid role of "constitutional" monarch. The contrast with his former key position may have enhanced his apprehensions that the Nepali Congress leadership was fundamentally unsympathetic to the institution of monarchy and was plotting its eventual abolition.

Whatever the King's motivations may have been, his actions were both drastic and effective. On December 15, 1960, the Nepali Congress ministers then in Kathmandu were arrested, the cabinet dismissed, and the Parliament dissolved. Sections of the 1959 Constitution were suspended—in accordance with its own provisions—and another period of direct rule commenced. A new cabinet, composed of a few ex-Nepali Congressmen and independents, was appointed, in which the King functioned as *de facto* prime minister.

With the discard of parliamentary democracy, King Mahendra renewed his experimentations with political institutions aimed at preserving the central role of the monarchy in the process of government. These events were not accepted without protest. Serious disorders were rife throughout Nepal in 1961 and 1962, mostly directed by Nepali Congress leaders in exile in India. The Sino-Indian border war of October-November, 1962, however, brought this resistance campaign to a sudden halt, and no major challenges to the royal regime have subsequently emerged. The King's new political system, termed "Panchayat Raj," was formalized in a new constitution bestowed on the country in December, 1962. While there have been numerous ministerial changes thereafter, none of these marked any significant changes in the government's internal and external policies, which are in a real sense the ultimate and exclusive prerogative of the Palace.

2. The Monarchy and Representative Institutions

The Monarchy

The political fortunes of the Shah dynasty, as even a brief glimpse into the modern history of Nepal will demonstrate, have fluctuated widely—ranging from periods of political impotence to periods of absolute authority. Indeed, it is difficult to define a "traditional" role for the monarch, not only because of these fluctuations but also because his role has probably been perceived differently by the various ethnic groups which constitute modern Nepal. Nevertheless, certain consistent features can be noted which have provided the legal basis for all of the political systems established since the conquest of Kathmandu Valley in 1769.

The Shah dynasty traces its ancestral line to highborn Rajputs who fled to the Himalayan region as a consequence of the Muslim conquest of Rajasthan in the fourteenth century. Their tradition is thus one of Hindu orthodoxy, imbued with Rajput (warrior) ideals and grounded upon time-honored Hindu concepts of monarchy. The Shah kings of Gorkha were no doubt forced to make a few concessions to local conditions, but the essential features of a Hindu monarchy were retained. According to traditional concepts, the king is an absolute monarch, possessing certain divine attributes appropriate to his status as a manifestation of Vishnu. The king's powers were, in theory, limited only by an obligation to uphold and maintain a Hindu polity as set forth in Hindu scriptures. In reality, his authority was often subjected to further limitation by the practical necessity of obtaining approbation from the Brahmans and of exacting obedience and loyalty from the Kshatriya nobility (*bharadar*).

To what extent the common people (*duniyadar*), many of whom had been incorporated only tenuously into a Hindu social structure, accepted this traditional concept of the monarch is not certain. But most of them had been ruled by Hindu dynasties for several centuries prior to the sudden expansion of the Gorkha kingdom throughout the hill area. Whether or not there were significant differences in attitudes toward kingship among Nepal's many communities, there is no reason to doubt a wide acceptance of absolutism and the sanctity of the king's status. These two themes have persisted to the present, and have been crucial in defining current popular attitudes toward the monarchy. It is significant that the provisions of the 1959 and 1962 constitutions, characterizing Nepal as a Hindu monarchy and stipulating that the ruler must be "an adherent of Aryan culture and a follower of the Hindu religion," have been accepted without outward protest by virtually all political groupings, including those who advocate extremist revolutionary principles.

Nevertheless, of the nine kings who have ascended the throne from the conquest of Kathmandu Valley to the present day, few indeed have been allowed to exercise the absolute powers under which Nepal has been ruled. From the time when the three-year-old Rana Bahadur Shah was placed on the throne in 1777 until the pattern was broken by the accession of King Mahendra in 1955, Nepal's kings have all ascended the throne as minors; furthermore, only one (the 17-year-old Surendra) was more than six years old. Young kings, attaining their majority at age eighteen, seldom found it easy to assert their royal prerogatives. Two who tried were soon thereafter forced to abdicate in favor of a minor son. Two others died under suspicious circumstances. From the time the Gorkha dynasty established its sway over the valley (1769) until King Mahendra came to the throne, the longest period during which the royal powers were actually in the hands of the king (that is, were neither held by regents nor surrendered to ministers) was the rule of King Rajendra. This monarch attained his majority in 1832 and retained his powers until 1846, but Rajendra's success was based on devious statecraft rather than on strong leadership. His reign not only was terminated by abdication, but the circumstances surrounding the abdication led step by step to the concentration of power in the hands of Jang Bahadur, until with the Sanad (royal order) of 1856, all effective political authority was deeded in perpetuity to the Ranas as hereditary prime ministers.

During the Rana period (1846–1951), the sovereignty of the king, although strictly nominal, continued to be acknowledged. All important documents required the customary Lal Mohar (royal seal—literally, "red stamp"),[1] although the gesture became purely symbolic, since the

[1] The Rana prime ministers later evolved a seal of their own, the Khadganishana, which was used on most official documents, including executive orders having the force of law. The royal seal, however, still was required for more important documents.

Rana prime minister controlled the royal seal. The sanctity of the king's status was given special emphasis, but the result—and presumable intent—was to prevent him from mingling with the people. Even in those religious ceremonies in which the king's presence was essential, he was frequently represented by a deputy. Only rarely did the reigning monarch leave his palace in public procession. To divert the royal family from any awkward interest in politics, entertainments of various kinds were provided within the palace. Each prime minister, in turn, arranged marriages whenever feasible between his own immediate branch of the Rana family and the heirs to the throne, thus hoping to strengthen his own position, safeguard the future of his sons and daughters, and bind the interests of the Shah dynasty more closely to his own. The royal family, preferring to make marital alliances with princely families in India, found this policy distasteful, but could offer only subtle and indirect resistance.

The treatment accorded the royal family reflected Rana realization that the most dangerous threat to their continued authority came from the monarchy. Why, then, did not the Ranas go one step further, depose the Shahs, and assume royal powers in their own name? At least two Rana prime ministers are reported to have given such a plan serious thought. Several considerations may have stayed their hands. Counterplots would surely follow, and the army's reaction could not be counted upon; but the principal deterrent may well have been opposition from within the Rana family itself. The hereditary prime ministership, which along with all other important offices passed from brother to brother in order of seniority, was an important part in the arrangements through which the first Rana consolidated his success. Neither then nor thereafter were the collateral branches of the family prepared to permit one of their number to seize the royal prerogatives for himself and his progeny, and relegate the rest to comparative obscurity. The royal family thus retained its nominal position, the span of the king's years increased significantly, and his titles were resplendent; but his actual position was that of royal prisoner, and the atmosphere surrounding him was contaminated with intrigue and suspicion.

The Rana system's century of existence has left a number of legacies which still are factors in contemporary Nepali politics. Among them must not be forgotten the effect which generations of suppression by the Ranas has left upon the royal family. Any monarch with such a personal and political history as this would be likely to approach with vigilance developments which might attenuate the authority of the crown, and to view with concern that which might adversely affect its status.

POST-1951 DEVELOPMENTS

The 1950 revolution was led by men who had a considerable popular following and had been strongly influenced by the nationalistic, democratic ideas prevalent in India. It culminated, in a matter of weeks, in the royal proclamation of February 18, 1951, which rescinded the Sanad of 1856 and thereby restored supreme authority to the crown. Most Nepali leaders, King Tribhuvan among them, assumed that the reinstatement of royal powers was a legal formality providing the base for the emergence of a democratic constitutional monarchy. The King several times reiterated his pledge that the details of the future government of Nepal would be determined by a popularly elected constituent assembly, and that while preparations for such an election were being made, democratic political and administrative procedures would be followed to the fullest possible extent. As an earnest of his intentions, the King, in the Interim Government of Nepal Act (1951), established in effect a king-in-council system under which the cabinet—a coalition in which popular forces were represented—served as the real center of political authority.

The shift from autocracy to a benign constitutional monarchy proved to be far less easy than had been expected in the first flush of enthusiasm. A bare two months after his restoration, a crisis forced the King to give added substance to his position as Commander-in-Chief by bringing the military under his direct command. By mid-1952, two cabinets had disintegrated and King Tribhuvan was forced to introduce, as a temporary expedient, a system of direct rule with an advisory council. A "Special Emergency Powers Act" was promulgated which suspended the clauses of the Interim Government of Nepal Act relevant to executive powers, and stated clearly that full executive authority was vested in the crown and could be exercised either directly or through royal appointees.

As soon as circumstances permitted, the king-in-council system was reinstituted (June, 1953) with the appointment of the second M. P. Koirala cabinet. But a series of High Court decisions which seriously undermined the cabinet's executive authority soon created a major political crisis. To end the near paralysis of governmental processes which ensued, the King issued a royal proclamation and three legislative amendments (February 13, 1954), the effects of which were to reaffirm the crown's supreme authority, and to place its right to delegate authority beyond the reach of the courts. This removal of all legal restrictions on the royal prerogatives permitted the cabinet to function again, but at the expense of the democratic system projected in the 1951 Interim Government of Nepal Act; the cabinet had perforce become totally dependent upon the crown.

The trend toward the centralization of power in the monarchy continued after King Mahendra's succession. One of his first acts (March, 1955) was the dismissal of the cabinet and the reinstitution of a period of direct rule in which he acted as his own prime minister. Later the King appointed a series of cabinets under successive party leaders, but he maintained a much more direct and immediate role in governmental affairs than his father had done. The earlier plan to leave the drafting of Nepal's constitution to an elected constituent assembly was also abandoned. King Mahendra decided to entrust the writing of a constitution to an appointed committee functioning under his direct supervision. The document which emerged specifically vested "executive power" in the king and reaffirmed his right to delegate that power "through ministers or other officers subordinate to him." Under certain circumstances the king was obligated to act on the advice of his ministers, but the extremely broad emergency powers granted to the crown left no effective restriction on the king. Indeed, the parliamentary institutions established by this constitution were abolished (December 15, 1960), in accordance with its own provisions.

In the interim period between the dismissal of the popularly elected Nepali Congress government in 1960 and the promulgation of the new constitution (December 16,

1962), King Mahendra was an absolute monarch both in law and in fact. Special legislation enacted during this period abrogated the few still valid restrictions placed on the powers of the crown after 1951. The 1962 Constitution does not so much limit these absolute powers as to establish the pattern according to which these powers will be exercised. The crown is the center around which all other institutions of government gravitate. Indeed, it is difficult to conceive of the successful functioning of the political system established under the 1962 Constitution in the absence of the direct participation of the monarch in administration and decision-making.

Constitutional monarchy has thus been given a basically different interpretation which distinguishes it from the system projected by King Tribhuvan and the leaders of the revolution of 1950. King Tribhuvan had preferred to keep the crown as free as possible from day-to-day political and administrative duties. Although forced to take up these functions by the series of crises which plagued his reign, his primary objective always appeared to be to create conditions which would enable him to retire once again to his role of constitutional monarch. King Mahendra, it would appear, views a passive role as akin to dereliction of duty, and considers the crown to be the one institution capable of providing the dynamic leadership required if Nepal is to maintain its national integrity and achieve rapid economic and political progress. This conviction was presumably strengthened by the brief experiment with constitutional monarchy in 1959–1960. In any event, few concessions to the principles of constitutional monarchy as it is known in the West were made in the 1962 constitutional system.

King Mahendra's political system is based upon a delicate balancing of administrative and political institutions, none of which is capable of acting on its own initiative even within the limited spheres of government nominally under its charge. This is perhaps most clearly demonstrated in the elaborate administrative apparatus which has been devised to give "guidance" and supervision to the panchayats at the regional and local levels. The Panchayat Ministry might seem to be the logical choice for the execution of this function, but in fact a number of other bodies have been created which effectively intrude upon the operation of the Ministry. The Zonal Commissioners, for instance, are appointed directly by the king and are, in the real sense, responsible to the king rather than the Central Secretariat. The National Guidance Council and the various tour commissions, also appointed by the king, have occasionally intruded into the area of the Panchayat Ministry without benefit of a consultation process. The result has been that even on comparatively minor administrative matters the lines of administrative and political authority are so intricately interwoven that they can be manipulated and untangled successfully at one level only—the Palace.

Here is the sharpest criticism leveled at the current system. It is widely conceded that the times require a strong guiding hand. The disagreement is over the appropriateness of the crown for this particular function. The crown, as an essential symbol of national unity, should, it is argued, remain above partisan politics. In the past, there were interposed between the crown and the public other institutions which in periods of crisis could assume full responsibility for errors or miscalculations, leaving the reputation of the monarchy unsullied. Today, the initiative and determination with which King Mahendra functions in the political sphere, and his recognized status as the focal point in the new political and administrative system, have fundamentally altered the situation. The king must now take action directly and in the name of the crown in matters for which other institutions had previously borne the responsibility. Thus, to a greater extent than ever before, the future of the monarchy is intertwined with that of the constitutional system, and, furthermore, with a constitutional system which can be operated effectively only by a strong, vigorous monarch. No alternative institutions exist within this system which could serve effectively in any interim period during which the crown might be incapable of assuming direction, since King Mahendra's system requires the delicate balancing of institutions one against another. Such a system, if kept in balance, assures the pre-eminence of the crown, but in any severe crisis or period of transition, might well throw an insupportable burden upon the monarchy as a viable institution.

The view that in our times the monarchical form of government had become an anachronism doomed to early extinction, although widely held, has been proved premature by the course of events in Asia since World War II. Several Asian ruling monarchs, including King Mahendra of Nepal, have demonstrated both the determination and the capacity to transform a tradition-encrusted institution into an agency of modernization and a fulcrum for nation-building activities. In Nepal the monarchy, because of its unique history, possessed the best of two worlds: it represented the continuity of tradition and yet it had been the spearhead of "revolution" against tyranny. King Mahendra was able to make effective use of the large legacy of loyalty and good will which he inherited from his predecessor, King Tribhuvan, the "Father of Democracy" in Nepal.

Despite widespread recognition that King Mahendra is a remarkably successful ruler, it seems probable that his achievements have, if anything, intensified the weakness basic to the monarchy as an institution—its dependence upon the hereditary principle to solve the succession problem. The political system which he devised demands of the monarch both astuteness and determination to rule rather than merely reign. Can such a system reasonably be expected to survive his eventual removal from the scene? Few well-informed Nepalis think it can, as evidenced at the time of Mahendra's heart attack in 1968. Many are doubtful about the future of the monarchy itself. Circumstances gave King Mahendra nearly a decade in which to master the intricacies of Nepali politics before having to make certain basic decisions; his successor is unlikely to have a similar period of grace. Further, given the complexity and demanding nature of the system he will inherit, the latitude for error may prove excessively narrow, especially if the new monarch embarks on his task untrained, untried, and inexperienced. The collapse of the "Basic Democracies" system in Pakistan once President Ayub had lost the physical capacity to exert dynamic leadership may hold a portent for Nepal.

In any event, with the spread of education and the opening of new employment opportunities, the effectiveness of the crown as unifier of the nation appears likely to require a shift in emphasis. The future of the monarchy may depend less on the monarch's ability to rule than on his capacity to share power on reasonable and mutually acceptable terms. Whether a lasting political system could be developed from "partyless panchayat democracy" either by King Mahendra or his successor remains open to serious question.

Representative Institutions

Although the history of parliamentary institutions in Nepal has been confined largely to the period since the 1950–1951 revolution, a few tentative, if ineffectual, steps in this direction were attempted during the Rana regime. That the prestige of British institutions underlay these earlier efforts is clear, but Nepali leaders were not necessarily bent solely on emulation. The desire to win British approval and consequent backing in internal power struggles appears also to have played its part in the transplanting of alien political institutions into Nepal.

The earliest attempt of which we have knowledge was made by the first Rana Prime Minister, Jang Bahadur, after his visit of 1850–1851 to England and France. On his return, he appointed a parliamentary office to prepare the foundations for the introduction of a parliamentary system. Nothing came of this proposal, however, owing to the opposition of Jang Bahadur's brothers and the absence of support, if not actual mistrust, of most other groups of political importance. It was nearly seven decades before another Rana Prime Minister, Chandra Shamsher, took any further initiative in the direction of popular government. He called a meeting of the most prominent members of the Rana family to discuss the introduction of constitutional change, but the response was so overwhelmingly unfavorable that the idea was dropped.

These first two attempts were undertaken by exceptionally strong and shrewd rulers. The most serious effort in the direction of parliamentarism, however, came in the last years of the Rana regime, with the succession of Padma Shamsher, a man who lacked strong family backing among the Ranas. Padma Shamsher appears to have attempted to rally the support of the royal family and generally dissident political elements behind a reform program. In 1947, he appointed a Reforms Committee which was instructed to prepare a draft constitution in consultation with advisers from newly independent India. On January 26, 1948, Padma Shamsher presented this first constitution to the country. Before the law could go into effect, however, Padma Shamsher had retired to India and "abdicated"—reportedly under heavy Rana pressure. His successor, Mohan Shamsher, had opposed the constitution, and in effect set it aside. By September, 1950, however, the internal and external situation had grown so serious that Mohan Shamsher, in a vain endeavor to stem the course of political disintegration, decided to resurrect the 1948 Constitution. Two months later, however, a revolution broke out, and in February, 1951, the Rana regime and its constitutional system were discarded simultaneously.

Despite the brief span of its existence, the 1948 Constitution deserves some attention, for it would appear to have exercised a strong influence on current political and institutional developments in Nepal. Even the words with which Padma Shamsher introduced the 1948 Constitution have a familiar ring to students of contemporary Nepali politics. The Rana Prime Minister had declared:

We have tried to mould the elective system of the west to the Panchayat system, which is an essential part of our heritage and culture. . . . It is the government's desire that all good, able and energetic elected representatives of the people should come to the centre, and co-operate with the government, but if would be very unfortunate if the introduction of political elections should lead to quarrels or disorder in the country. . . . It is not the intention of the government that the country should be thrown into the vortex of the party system, and the government will never lend its encouragement to the habit of bringing about the election of any candidate by the strength of party machinery rather than by his own ability and eligibility.[2]

These could just as well be the words of King Mahendra in his current exhortations on the virtues of "partyless panchayat democracy."

The main features of the 1948 Constitution were: (1) a three-tiered electoral system—primary, district, and national—in which the primary panchayat unit was to be elected by universal suffrage, and the higher levels indirectly from among the members of the next lower body; (2) a bicameral national parliament whose upper house (Bharadari Sabha) was to be appointed by the Rana prime minister and to enjoy equal powers with the lower house; (3) strict limitations on the subjects which the parliament could take under consideration; (4) reservation of final legislative powers to the Rana prime minister, who was also given comprehensive emergency powers; and (5) a Council of Ministers responsible to the prime minister rather than to parliament.

The 1948 Constitution diminished only slightly the political powers of the autocratic Rana prime ministers. Nevertheless, insofar as it permitted the trappings of office

[2] *Free English Rendering of the Government of Nepal Act, 2004 Sambat, Together with the Inaugural Speech of His Highness Maharaja Padma Shum Shere Jung Bahadur Rana* (Kathmandu, 1947), p. 7.

to be shared with the elected representatives of the people, it would have significantly diluted the Rana monopoly of social prestige, and conceivably could have become an opening wedge to an eventual sharing of political power. The dominant branch of the Rana family moved quietly to avert this threat in 1948, only to find themselves in a far worse plight a scant two years later. Their willingness in 1950 to give effect to the 1948 Constitution could no longer stem the tide. The 1950 revolution resulted in drastic changes in the Nepali constitutional system. A new organic law, the Interim Government of Nepal Act, was promulgated by King Tribhuvan in April, 1951, to serve until a constituent assembly could be elected and a new constitution framed.

The 1951 Act was concerned primarily with the executive aspect of government rather than with representative institutions. The most significant provision in this document was the stipulation that the executive powers were vested in the king *and* his council of ministers, and were to be exercised by the king "in accordance with the advice of his ministers." There was, thus, no equivalent of the Rana prime minister in the 1951 system. Indeed, lack of any real center of administrative and executive authority was one of the most critical weaknesses of the system.

By the end of 1951 it had become evident that the election of a constituent assembly was likely to be delayed for several years, owing both to technical and political factors, and that an interim arrangement was required for the association of "popular" representatives with the government. In April, 1952, therefore, an amendment to the Interim Government of Nepal Act was approved, providing for an Advisory Assembly appointed by the king. As its name implied, the Assembly was an advisory body whose limited legislative powers could easily be contravened by either king or cabinet. The absence of responsibility encouraged the Assembly to indulge in bursts of oratory which were often embarrassing to the government without being constructive in character. This first Assembly was hastily prorogued, as was a second Advisory Assembly in 1955, and for similar reasons. Indeed, during most of the period from 1951 to the appointment of a third Assembly in 1958, the provisions of the 1951 Act with respect to the Assembly were simply ignored by the executive branch.

The Interim Government of Nepal Act, as amended, represented an attempt to establish a constitutional monarchy based on a limited application of the principles of parliamentary democracy, but lacking certain basic ingredients of a parliamentary system. The advisory assemblies, deprived of any effective function, adopted a gadfly role. The relation between the king and his council of ministers, although expressed in terms of royal action on ministerial advice, was in essence unparliamentary, since the ministers were solely responsible to the king and could be removed at his discretion. Underlying this system was a profound paradox: it was unworkable without strong mutual trust between the sovereign and his cabinet, and yet many of its provisions were in themselves evidence of a fundamental absence of royal confidence in the ministry. King Tribhuvan appears to have had a genuine desire to reign as a constitutional monarch and leave governing powers largely in the hands of his ministers, but the sudden withdrawal of autocratic control had left the field open to the competing ambitions of various untested aspirants to leadership. In this situation, only the monarch was in a position to exert a unifying influence. King Trib-huvan, however reluctantly, was more than once forced to intervene. The same compulsion toward intervention con-tinued to operate under King Mahendra, but the reluc-tance could no longer be taken for granted.

When King Mahendra succeeded to the throne in 1955 it was believed that he assumed at the same time his fa-ther's commitment to a popularly elected constituent as-sembly. This may have been so in 1955, but by 1957 the instability displayed by successive cabinets provided little ground for confidence that a constituent assembly would be able to perform its task with efficiency or dispatch, and at the same time preserve the status and powers of the monarchy. King Mahendra came to the conclusion that the best procedure would be to present a constitution to the people, and to proceed under its provisions with elec-tions not for a constituent assembly but for a parliament. Meanwhile he arranged for the "election" of a third Advi-sory Assembly in 1958. In these elections each district was called upon to nominate a number of candidates at a pub-lic meeting, from among whom the king appointed the As-sembly. If this expedient was indeed intended, as is some-times charged, to obviate any constitutional change, the effort was a signal failure. The response from political leaders throughout Nepal was increased clamor for a full-fledged parliamentary system as envisaged by King Trib-huvan. In the end, King Mahendra bestowed a Constitu-tion upon the country in February, 1959—the work of a drafting committee which had functioned under his direct supervision.

The 1959 Constitution was in most respects modeled upon the British constitutional system as modified and adapted by India. All the usual characteristics of parliamentary democracy, including the concept of ministerial responsibility to the legislature, were in evidence, although occasionally in somewhat diluted form. The emergency powers granted the Head of State (i.e., the king) were more extensive than is normal in democratic constitutions, but those provisions were widely accepted as necessary, given Nepal's political instability. The general expectation was that those powers would be exercised only upon the advice of the cabinet, as is the case in India and the United Kingdom.

For the first twenty months of its existence, the Constitution appeared to be functioning in normal parliamentary fashion. During the initial phase, King Mahendra's conduct as constitutional monarch appeared to be exemplary, and the Cabinet was the real center of executive authority. All things considered, the democratic experiment proceeded smoothly, and there was reason to hope that the extreme instability that had marked all aspects of government since 1951 was finally at an end.

This phase of Nepal's constitutional development came to an abrupt halt on December 15, 1960, with the dismissal of the Nepali Congress government and the imprisonment of its members. The most reasonable interpretation of the trend of developments during the next twelve months was that King Mahendra had reached the decision that parliamentary democracy as incorporated in the 1959 Constitution should be discarded, but had not come to a settled conclusion as to what should replace it. Gradually, however, the basic format of a new political structure began to emerge until, in December, 1962, a new constitutional ordinance was promulgated by the King. As noted above, this constitution bears a distinct resemblance in some respects to the Rana Constitution of 1948. It also has at least some superficial resemblance to Panchayati Raj in India, and owes some of its features to other experiments such as Indonesia's "National Guidance," Pakistan's "Basic Democracy," and the "Class Organization" systems of Egypt and Yugoslavia.

PANCHAYAT RAJ

Even before the promulgation of the 1962 constitutional ordinance, however, several of the institutions upon which the new system was based had already started functioning. Panchayats, class and professional organizations, and the National Guidance Ministry, for example, had been established in 1961 as separate, although interdependent, institutions. To this basic structure were appended several peripheral institutions such as the Council of State (Raj Sabha), the tour commissions (*daudaha*), and the National Guidance Council with important although largely undefined functions. Initially the interrelations between these institutions seemed contrived, but gradually they have been welded into what is, at least in theory, a coherent and integrated system of government.[3]

The system as a whole is termed Panchayat Raj (government by panchayats), and it is with this latter institution that an analysis of the 1962 political system will begin. In Nepal, as in India, the term "panchayat" is of hoary origin and is a significant feature of traditional

[3] For a detailed description and analysis of the origin, functions, and powers of these institutions, see Bhuwan Lal Joshi and Leo E. Rose, *Democratic Innovations in Nepal: A Case Study of Political Acculturation* (Berkeley, 1966), pp. 395–419.

Hindu cultural ethos. Again, as in India, panchayats are elusive institutions historically, defying definition in modern political terms. In Nepal, traditional panchayats have been for the most part associated with castes, and particularly with jurisdiction over caste matters. They may also at times have carried out what are essentially political functions as well, but they were not in any real sense a unit of government in the traditional village system except as spokesmen for the castes within the village structure. What is being established in Nepal, therefore, is in fundamental respects a new political institution, bearing a traditional and prestige-laden name.

The panchayat system, as outlined in the 1962 Constitution and amended in 1967, has been organized on a three-tier structure. On the lowest (primary) level are the village (*gram*) and town (*nagar*) panchayats; superimposed on these are district (*zilla*) panchayats, one for each of the 75 development districts.[4] Finally, at the highest level, is the national (*rashtriya*) panchayat—the "parliament" under Panchayat Raj. The primary units alone are popularly elected. All other panchayats are elected by the level directly below from among its own members, thus providing, at least in theory, a pyramidal structure on a popular base. Local elections were held throughout Nepal in 1962, and village and town panchayats were set up. Once these were functioning, district panchayats were elected, and then in rapidly progressing order, zonal and national pan-

[4] The 1962 Constitution had also provided for fourteen zonal (*anchal*) panchayats. The 1967 amendment to the Constitution, however, replaced this body with *anchal* committees consisting of the chairmen of district panchayats, class and professional organizations, and up to five members nominated by the king.

chayats were established. By April, 1963, the entire pan-chayat system was functioning, a remarkable example of the speed and efficiency with which the Nepali bureau-cracy can move when provided with the necessary author-ity and incentive.

The panchayat system supposedly represents an attempt to decentralize both political power and the governmental process, and is frequently defended as a "higher" form of democracy than "western-style" democracy. Whatever the ultimate character of the system may be, it is obvious from the 1962 Constitution and supplementary legislation that for the immediate future a minimum degree of decentrali-zation is projected. Indeed, the 1962 village and town pan-chayat legislation is less liberal, particularly with respect to the form and extent of controls exercised by the central government, than laws that had been previously enacted on these same subjects. Political power is still strongly cen-tralized in Nepal, and no real intention to decentralize basic decision-making functions is yet evident. The new panchayat system would seem at this stage to constitute an attempt to rationalize the administrative process by creat-ing viable institutions where serious gaps had previously existed, thus providing the basis for a truly national ad-ministrative system as well as agencies through which eco-nomic development programs could be implemented.

The National Panchayat, as the parliament in the 1962 constitutional system, is destined to play a key role in the functioning of the panchayat system, and is the institution upon which most political interest has centered. Indeed, much of the participation at other levels of the panchayat system and the class and professional organizations would appear to be directly related to their character as vehicles for election to the National Panchayat. Under the new electoral system, ninety of the members of the National Panchayat are elected by the Zonal Assemblies, fifteen by the national conferences of the class and professional organizations, and four from graduate constituencies composed of Nepali citizens who have obtained a Bachelor's degree in a western-style college or a Shastri in a Sanskritic institution. The king has also reserved the power to nominate a certain number, not to exceed fifteen per cent of the elected membership.

The provisions of the 1962 Constitution reflect a considerable expansion of royal prerogatives over the 1959 law. This is evident in various contexts: the legislative process; the relationship of the Council of Ministers with respect to the crown and to the legislature; and the comprehensive "emergency" and special powers granted to the king. Not only has the crown retained an irreversible veto power over all legislation, but certain procedures are also specified under which legislation can be promulgated from the throne without the approval of the National Panchayat. The ministers are appointed by the king from among the members of the National Panchayat,[5] but are responsible only to the king and can be dismissed by the king without reference to any support they may enjoy in the legislature. The National Panchayat can, by a two-thirds majority vote, pass a no-confidence resolution

[5] The king may appoint ministers who are not members of the National Panchayat, but they must become members of that body within six months. This requirement does not impose an effective limitation on the king's choice of ministers, however, as he also has the power to appoint a certain percentage of the membership of the National Panchayat.

against any minister, but not against the ministry as a unit. This action has only the force of a recommendation, moreover, and is not binding upon the king. The "emergency" powers granted the king are so comprehensive and the nominal legal limitations placed on their exercise are, in the Nepali context, so ineffectual, that the king could suspend, amend, or discard the 1962 Constitution as easily as he did that of 1959.

But perhaps the policy toward political parties and organizations is more indicative of the spirit of the 1962 Constitution than are the legal provisions per se. A ban on political parties and organizations has been incorporated as an essential feature of Panchayat Raj. As no form of political alignment is permitted, the National Panchayat's significance as a representative institution and a legislative body has been seriously compromised. In some respects it has been assigned a less significant role than the earlier advisory assemblies with their irresponsible but well-publicized oratory and their party ties to members of the Council of Ministers. Because of a unique provision in the 1962 Constitution which specifies that all sessions of the National Panchayat must be held *in camera* unless royal permission is granted for an open meeting, it is difficult to appraise the influence of this body on the legislative process. According to reports, amendments have been accepted on several bills introduced by the ministers, and on at least one occasion a bill was actually withdrawn because of the expectation of substantial opposition in the National Panchayat. But these are the exception to the general rule, which is acceptance of whatever is submitted in essentially its original form and an extreme reluctance to participate in the legislative process through the introduction of private members' bills.

By and large, therefore, the National Panchayat has more the character of a consultative body whose opinion is solicited by the king and his ministers than a real legislature. While many members may be unhappy with this situation, it has not been considered expedient to raise such questions under prevailing political conditions. Criticism of the National Panchayat has been directed instead at a less significant—and thus safer—level: namely, the secret session provision which both the members and the public find irksome. This rule was introduced presumably with the experience of the advisory assemblies in mind, and in particular their capacity for disruption and parochialism. Disunity may have been contained thereby, but it is by no means clear that genuine unity has been promoted. Indeed, it may have had the opposite effect. Conditions have been created under which the selection of candidates for the National Panchayat and the devising of *ad hoc* alignments within that body are determined by personality and expediency rather than by programs or policies. And yet, at the same time, these political personalities have been denied the means of satisfaction they formerly enjoyed through the capacity to build a position of leadership through intensive public exposure. Whether national unity or national frustration has been fostered is debatable.

The class and professional organizations play a subsidiary but important role in Panchayat Raj as visualized by the king and his advisers. Prior to 1961, most such organizations in Nepal were connected directly or implicitly with the political parties. The ban on party activity thus led to a new approach toward affiliated organizations. Direct government sponsorship and supervision of these organizations was taken to be the most suitable solution, and in 1961, class and professional organizations of peasants, labor, women, students, youth, children, and ex-servicemen were established. Each of these organizations was guaranteed a monopoly in its respective sphere, and even peripheral organizations were brought within the confines of the system—e.g., all commercial associations had to function under the supervision of the labor organization, though they were allowed an autonomous organizational structure. Each of these bodies is organized on a hierarchical basis directly paralleling the structure of the panchayat system.

"Guided democracy" was the announced objective in establishing Panchayat Raj in Nepal. A National Guidance Ministry, to provide the necessary "guidance," was created in February, 1961, and under the new political structure was given an overwhelming array of duties and responsibilities. The Ministry's first assignment was the creation of the panchayats and the class and professional organizations. Once these bodies were functioning, the Ministry's duty was then to coordinate and supervise their activities, and to prevent them from encroaching upon each other's spheres or otherwise exceeding their proper functions.

With the election of the National Panchayat in April, 1963, the primary task of the National Guidance Ministry was considered to have been completed and the Ministry was abolished. This did not mark the end of "guidance," however, as the powers and functions of the National Guidance Ministry were transferred to the Panchayat

Ministry. In addition, a National Guidance Council was appointed by the King to exercise general supervision over the functioning of the panchayat system. The Council was established as an independent body outside the Secretariat, and the nature of its relationship with the Panchayat Ministry was ill defined. In theory, the Council was responsible for the formation of policy, but it failed to assert itself in this and other respects, and finally was abolished in April, 1967.

The 1962 Constitution also provided for the appointment by the king of a Raj Sabha (Council of State) to serve in an essentially advisory capacity. The Raj Sabha has two primary functions: to supervise succession to the throne in the event of the king's death or incapacity, and to serve as a consultative body whenever the king and the National Panchayat fail to agree on proposed legislation. In addition, a permanent committee consisting of from seven to fifteen members of the Raj Sabha can be appointed by the king to act in conjunction with the Steering Committee of the National Panchayat on specified occasions—in particular, during periods of national emergency and in the constitutional amendment process.

Just what the general role of the Raj Sabha is expected to be in the new political structure is still unclear. It is reminiscent, however, of the councils which King Mahendra appointed during earlier periods when he ruled through a cabinet but found it desirable to name another body with high prestige and few responsibilities. The King's appointments to the Raj Sabha have been primarily from among the ranks of ex-party and government leaders, Ranas, and royal kinsmen—persons best described as too important to be ignored, but considered unsuitable for one reason or another for responsible posts in the new political system. This heterogeneous body is broadly representative of the range of the political viewpoints which have found expression in Nepal, but it would have extreme difficulty in reaching a consensus without strong leadership from the Palace.

Another device of which King Mahendra has made considerable use is the tour commission (*daudaha*), an appointed body dispatched to an outlying region, usually with such broad discretionary powers as: (1) the supervision of all government offices in the area, including the authority to suspend higher-level officials and dismiss lower-level staff; (2) judicial authority equivalent to that of the District Court; and (3) the inspection of social and economic conditions, appraising development projects already begun, and recommending new programs. The device was not new, as similar commissions had been used by the Ranas as a regular part of their administrative system. Post-revolutionary governments had abandoned this practice until it was revived by King Mahendra in 1955, only to be dropped quietly as a result of protests both from party leaders and government officials. One of the first steps taken by the King after the December, 1960, coup, however, was the dispatch of tour commissions to various regions. Tour commissions were reappointed in 1962 at the time the panchayat system was being introduced, and again several times thereafter, usually in connection with panchayat development.

Are tour commissions likely to become a regular feature of Panchayat Raj? No legislation to this effect has as yet been enacted, and none is reported to be under consideration. But none is needed, as the commissions have always been appointed on an *ad hoc* basis by the Palace.[6] They have served to explain the King's objectives and programs to the people, and can probably be expected to continue as long as King Mahendra views them as a fruitful method for developing closer ties between the monarch and the people, and for providing him with more direct lines of communication with regional units of government.

It is as yet too early to speculate with any confidence upon the ultimate character of Panchayat Raj in Nepal. It may retain the essentially authoritarian character with which it began, or it may gradually be liberalized. As the system now stands, certain incongruities indicate where troublesome consequences may well be expected unless suitable remedies can be found. Outstanding among these incongruities is the vocal emphasis being laid upon the principles of political decentralization when both the external and internal situation demand increasing centralization if political unity and economic progress are to be achieved. Concessions to local, regional, and ethnic sentiments may be unavoidable, but it is questionable whether they should be enshrined within the constitutional system. Further, these concessions to the outlying regions stand in sharp contrast to the absence of concessions to the young

[6] In April, 1966, a special unit of the Home and Panchayat Ministry was formed to conduct frequent tours of the zones. These differed from the earlier tour commissions in two important aspects: (1) the extent of their powers, and (2) the fact that they functioned under the Ministry rather than directly under the king. That this unit was not intended to replace the older style commissions became evident in 1966 and 1968 when "high-powered" tour commissions headed by National Panchayat members and including former zonal commissioners and district judges were appointed.

intellectuals and budding political activists of the capital. To some extent this too may have been inevitable, since there is an understandably wide gulf between their outlook on the world and that of the Palace. Nevertheless, it is hard to believe that the institutional forms which had received the support of these young intellectuals were wholly irreconcilable with the nation-building objectives of the royal regime. Some way to bring all these forces together is well worth the search; for unless the panchayat and class and professional organization systems can somehow develop an intrinsic strength of their own, the gap between the ideal and the real may eventually prove too great a strain upon the constitutional fabric.

3. The Administrative and Judicial Systems

Nepalis, in commenting upon the effect of the revolution on administration, frequently sum it up in such terms as these: the Rana system was both "primitive" and "feudal," but once a decision was reached, it was carried out; the bureaucracy has now been "modernized," but policy decisions, when finally forthcoming, are seldom implemented with any determination or thoroughness. This comparison points up real weaknesses in the current system, but it is unrealistic and unfair in ignoring the drastic changes that have been introduced in the objectives of administration in the post-Rana period. The Ranas viewed the bureaucracy primarily as an instrument for the preservation of their political authority and for the collection of revenue—functions that required only a relatively simple administrative operation. The post-1951 political systems, with their goal of a modern welfare society, require a much more complex organizational structure. Unfortunately, the changes in objectives and structure have not been accompanied by concomitant changes in methods of operation. The heritage of the traditional administrative system is a major factor shaping the bureaucracy, and some of its basic characteristics are still evident, if in somewhat altered form.

The pre-1951 administrative system directly reflected the ruling family's hierarchical structure. At the top of the pyramid was the prime minister, who had been granted absolute administrative authority by the king. The management of state affairs was shared with the more important Ranas under a system in which the highest military and civil posts normally devolved automatically in accordance with rank on the roll of succession or relationship to the current prime minister. Lower ranking Ranas and non-Ranas were barred from posts above a certain grade, a fact which had serious consequences in the immediate post-revolutionary period when few administrators with policy-making experience were available to replace the Ranas.

The Rana prime minister was assured control over the administration by the procedure under which the appointments of all officials were reaffirmed annually—the *pajani* ceremony. This system was abolished in the administrative reforms of 1951 in the interests of providing civil servants with a broader degree of job security. Actually, however, the results were not those intended. Under the old system, government employees were assured at least limited security of tenure, since it was unusual to dismiss an official except at the time of the annual *pajani*. In post-1951 Nepal on the other hand, government servants have often been dismissed without notice and without any opportunity for appeal. Nevertheless, the situation under both regimes is broadly similar in that neither had institutionalized procedures which effectively protected civil servants from arbitrary dismissal.

The financial system under the Rana regime was also distinctly non-modern, since all state revenues were the personal income of the prime minister, who had to approve all expenditures. Nepal never had a public budget until after the fall of the Rana regime, and then only in the most rudimentary form. A substantial proportion of the revenue collected by the Rana regime was not used for governmental purposes, but was instead invested outside of Nepal to ensure the prime minister and his family against economic disaster in case the ever-volatile trend of Nepali politics should suddenly turn unfavorable.

The comparative simplicity of administrative objectives under the Ranas did not result in a simple administrative structure, however. No attempt was ever made to rationalize the division of functions between departments, which had often been established on an *ad hoc* basis to carry out a particular task, only to be retained after its completion. There were, for example, an Old Roads Department, a New Roads Department, a department for roads in the hills and Terai, and two separate departments responsible for roads in Kathmandu Valley. The jurisdictional confusion emanating from such a structure would have made operation impossible if administrative authority had not been effectively centralized in the hands of the prime minister who, moreover, usually made decisions personally. While the system would appall the modern student of public administration, it was not in point of fact as unworkable as might seem, given the limited objectives of administration.

The Central Secretariat

The overthrow of the Ranas led inevitably to major changes in the structure of the administrative system. These structural changes were not accompanied by equally significant changes in the bureaucracy's operating principles, however. Many of the civil servants—of necessity holdovers from the Rana period—tended to adhere staunchly to well-tried and well-known procedures. The high degree of centralization of authority and responsibility that had characterized the Rana regime was not perceptibly diminished; it merely lost the fulcrum which had enabled the system to function at all. In theory, the absolute authority of the Rana regime was transferred back to the crown, but while King Tribhuvan was on the throne he preferred to delegate these powers to a cabinet. Power, while still centralized, was now divided among several ministers rather than concentrated in the hands of the prime minister, causing extreme confusion as to the limits of ministerial jurisdiction.

Officials below the ministerial level continued to display reluctance to assume decision-making responsibilities, even in matters that did not involve substantive policy issues. The frequency of ministerial changes and the instability of the political party system further complicated the administrative task. Several reforms were attempted but had only limited impact. A Central Secretariat was established and a Public Service Commission was appointed with nominal authority to regulate appointments to the government service and to standardize rules of procedure and operation. Little progress was made in either direction, however. Indeed, the rules of procedure (*ains* and *sawals*) that had been formulated for the various departments during the Rana period were retained intact until 1963, effectively subverting the efforts toward procedural reforms that were made sporadically in the interim.

After the ascent of King Mahendra to the throne in

1955, the pace of administrative reorganization was quickened. The Secretariat was reorganized, and a civil service law was enacted. An Organizations and Methods Department was established in 1956 to supervise administrative reorganization and to make periodic reviews of departmental operating procedures. The Tanka Prasad government (1956–1957) commenced a program under which all government employees were to be "screened," after which those retained in service would be given some form of job security. Before this process was completed, however, the cabinet fell and the program was set aside until the advent of the elected Nepali Congress government in 1959. The following year the Central Secretariat was reorganized into twelve ministries: Home Affairs, Foreign Affairs, Forests and Agriculture, Industry and Commerce, Public Works, Transport and Communication, Education, Finance, Law and Justice, Planning and Development, Health, Irrigation and Power, Defense, and the Panchayat Ministry. After the dismissal of the Nepali Congress ministry in December, 1960, the King left the Secretariat structure virtually intact, but he pushed through a personnel reorganization program under which a large number of government servants were dismissed without reference to existing legislation or to the nominal prerogatives of the Public Service Commission.

Many of the weaknesses which had hampered administration in the early post-revolution years are still in evidence, despite the many attempts to eliminate them through reform and reorganization. The decision-making process continues to be highly confused, and the locus of responsibility for decisions is often difficult to determine. The enlarged administrative structure and the more complex nature of the problems with which the government is now concerned make it virtually impossible for the king to function effectively in the style of the Rana prime ministers, but, in essence, that is what is expected of him. No other official is prepared or, indeed, is in a position to assume responsibility for even comparatively minor matters which can more safely be pushed to the Palace for a final decision. Where this procedure is not feasible, the tendency is to form *ad hoc* committees within the Central Secretariat to consider a question, thus reducing individual responsibility, but slowing down the decision-making process.

Equally serious is the lack of effective implementation of decisions once they have been made. The obviously faulty structure of the administrative machinery is only one of the difficulties involved. More important, perhaps, is the apparent tendency for upper-level officials to quietly sabotage policy decisions at the implementation stage when these are considered to run contrary to their personal, family, or class interests. Deprived of any direct role in the formulation of policy, these officials have found it both safer and more effective to express their opposition in this way, rather than take the risk of obtruding unwelcome opinions while the decision is being reached. This process is not confined to internal administrative matters, but is also evident in the programs undertaken in cooperation with foreign aid agencies.

Certain weaknesses exhibited by the Central Secretariat are directly traceable to the Rana heritage. The general attitude toward financial expenditures is a case in point, as it still has some aspects associated more with familial practices than with a modern bureaucratic operation.

There have been instances in which programs have been planned, approved, and sometimes even put into operation before it was determined whether the requisite financial resources were available. Moreover, as during the Rana period, funds continue to be disbursed to individual officials rather than to departments, thus placing a burdensome responsibilty on the persons involved, who often tend to be overcautious in approving expenditures to the detriment of approved programs. Reporting and auditing procedures are unsatisfactory both as to method of operation and objectives. The budget sometimes appears to be treated as a general guide, to be ignored when inconvenient, rather than as a basic framework within which government operations should be made to fit. This is particularly the case for the Palace, which has on occasion redirected the utilization of funds on the spur of the moment without proper consideration of the impact on the total budget.

Other aspects of the Rana administrative system are also still evident. Prior to 1950, for instance, it was normal for each of the higher Rana officials to have his own little *durbar* (i.e., court) at which his "clients" in the government service would present themselves each morning to pay their respects. This practice, known as the *chakari* system, involved the establishment of mutual obligations between the Ranas and their followers. The procedures are no longer as elaborate and stylized, but a *chakari*-type relationship between high secretariat officials and their subordinates is still a common practice. This is, of course, not unique to Nepal by any means, but it is perhaps more formalized and extensive there than elsewhere. A high official is said to be evaluated by the lower ranks of the bureaucracy more by his success in protecting and advancing his clients than in the skill and efficiency with which he performs his duties.

This sophisticated variation of the Hindu *jajmani* system, involving a complicated exchange of obligations, has also served to restrict access to the middle and higher levels of the bureaucracy to members of elite families. During the Rana period, government positions were monopolized by some two hundred "client families"—mostly Kathmandu-based Brahmans and Kshatriyas but with a few Newari Shresthas included. These three high-caste groups still provide 80–90 per cent of the personnel at the middle and higher levels of the bureaucracy. Outgroup members from other social classes and regions—and particularly the Terai—experience severe handicaps first in obtaining appointment to the service and then in winning promotions, partly because of their lack of a client relationship. Resentment against this form of discrimination is very strong in certain regions and among some newly politicized groups in Nepal.

Perhaps the greatest obstacle to the improvement of the administrative system, however, is the lack of security of tenure at any level of the secretariat. Since 1955 there have been several major purges of the civil service during which thousands of government employees have been dismissed for essentially political reasons, and usually in a manner inconsistent with established rules. The powers of the Public Service Commission have been steadily eroded to a point where today that body is completely excluded from any role in the appointment and dismissal of higher-level officers and is often ignored at the lower levels as well. The effect on the morale of civil servants is evident.

A large number of talented young Nepalis, who have gained an expertise in various fields through education at home and abroad, often find their training to be nearly irrelevant once they join the government service. A successful civil service career has less to do with the quality of work performed than with the capacity to foresee political trends and to align with the victorious faction. The evident enthusiasm and idealism with which these young men enter the government usually dissipates rapidly, and many of them end up as sad but cynical practitioners of the expedient within a very short time.

Finally, the whole approach to administrative reorganization has been sporadic rather than systematic, with the result that the few reforms effected have had minimal impact. One change is introduced here, another there, but no truly rational and coherent process of reform can be discerned. Moreover, the impetus for procedural changes has often stemmed from foreign advisors or from Nepalis who have been trained in public administrations abroad, and the new system recommended for adoption therefore tends to be modelled directly after those in Western bureaucracies. All too often these new procedures are incompatible with traditional Nepali social and moral concepts and are therefore virtually ignored. Instead of insisting upon an acceptance of Western concepts of responsibility and devolution of authority, it might well be more realistic to adapt, insofar as possible, the principles and objectives of modern administration to the existing pattern of values. This has not yet been tried, but there would seem to be no reason to assume that traditional Nepali values and attitudes are necessarily incompatible with the goal of an efficient administration. This more imaginative approach might avoid many of the chronic frustrations and failures that have afflicted the post-1951 programs directed at administrative reform.

THE PALACE SECRETARIAT

No study of the central administrative structure in Nepal would be complete without an analysis of the role of the Palace Secretariat. While not formally part of the central bureaucracy, the Palace Secretariat nevertheless plays a crucial part in the administrative process. Indeed, in present-day Nepal, there are two centers of decision-making—the Palace Secretariat and the Central Secretariat—of which the former is by far the more important.

In the pre-Rana period (1769–1846), the royal palace was the hub of the administrative structure. At that time appointments to most official positions within the palace were the hereditary privilege of various noble, Brahman, and Newari families. With the transference of real power to the Rana family after 1846, the influence of the officials at the royal palace declined drastically, and the staff at the Rana prime minister's palace became the focus of administrative authority.

Following the 1950–1951 revolution, King Tribhuvan revamped and expanded his private secretariat. The hereditary principle for appointment to office was retained, but new recruits representing a variety of interest groups were added from time to time. King Tribhuvan, however, had not intended to develop an alternative administrative center with important decision-making functions. The Palace Secretariat was used essentially as a relay station between the king and the government, even during the direct rule period in 1952–1953.

After the accession of King Mahendra to the throne in 1955 and the institution of a second period of direct rule, the Palace Secretariat was expanded and its role underwent a fundamental change. To the small core of personal secretaries, mostly members of a Newari family that had traditionally served this function, and the Brahman royal priests and astrological technicians, were added a group of military attachés to assist the king in his capacity as supreme commander in chief of the Nepal Army and a palace intelligence unit. In this interim period (1955–1959) the Palace Secretariat functioned as a supragovernment body, using the Central Secretariat mainly as an instrument for the transmittal and implementation of decisions.

The introduction of parliamentary democracy in 1959 reversed this process, and the Palace Secretariat was once again relegated to a secondary role, apparently with King Mahendra's consent. The palace officials accepted their downgrading with ill-concealed resentment, but there was little they could do about it. With the imprisonment of B. P. Koirala and his colleagues in December, 1960, however, the Palace Secretariat regained a pre-eminent position within the Nepali administrative system, functioning not only as the channel of communication between the Central Secretariat and the king but also, until 1966, as the secretariat for the Council of Ministers.

As the procurer, purveyor, and censor of all communications channelled to the king, the Palace Secretariat is in a highly strategic position in the decision-making process. The criteria employed by the Palace Secretariat in soliciting information, and the biases which influence their selection of data to be placed in the transmission channel, have doubtless played a vital part in the determination of public policy in Nepal. King Mahendra appears to be fully aware of the limitations on his own freedom of action inherent in this situation. He has developed a variety of techniques to test and validate the reports he receives through the palace communication network, including personal walking tours among the people, the periodic dispatch of "tour commissions" throughout the country that report back directly to him, and the careful solicitation of the views of the concerned interest groups on subjects under consideration. Nevertheless, it is still the Palace Secretariat that operates at the focus of the political and administrative process, and its predominance over other government bodies in Nepal is still recognized and accepted.

Regional Administration

The rapid expansion of the dominions of the Shah dynasty in the latter half of the eighteenth century brought a large conglomeration of petty principalities under the authority of the Kathmandu government. The manner of their absorption by the Gorkha rulers determined their position within the newly evolving political structure, and has continued to influence the character of the regional government system in Nepal down to the present day. Those principalities that resisted the Gorkha onslaught were directly absorbed and were governed by officials deputed by and responsible to Kathmandu. The hill Rajas who allied themselves with the Shah rulers and aided the Gorkhas were, at least initially, allowed a fairly broad degree of autonomy within their own territory— now termed Rajyas. In eastern Nepal, the politically decentralized but powerful Kirati and Limbu communities were placed within a regional government system appointed by Kathmandu, although the privileges and powers of the local political elite were guaranteed. Other ethnic groups, such as the Thakalis and Sherpas in the northern border area and the Tharus in the Terai, were similarly allowed broad local autonomy under the general supervision of central government officials.

Once the authority of the Shah dynasty had been firmly established, however, a slow but steady process of centralization commenced. The vassal Rajas gradually had to surrender most of their prerogatives until by 1950 these had been reduced to the exercise of limited judicial functions, revenue collection, and the right to exact forced labor (*begar*). After 1951, the hill Rajas were gradually divested of the few privileges they had retained under the Ranas. In 1956, the forced labor system was officially abolished throughout Nepal including the Rajya areas. In 1960, the Nepali Congress government enacted legislation depriving the Rajas of their judicial and revenue collecting powers, and in the following year King Mahendra ordered the total abolition of the Rajya system. A few of the more important princely families were granted their titles to the third generation, but the rest were allowed to retain them only during the lifetime of the current Raja. These chiefs were all granted allowances which were to continue unless he abandoned Hinduism, became a citizen of a foreign country, violated the act abolishing Rajyas, or proved to be (in the opinion of the king), a person of bad character.

Change within the centrally administered areas followed a slow, somewhat parallel course. These areas were reorganized on several occasions under the Shah kings and the Ranas, until by 1950 there were thirty-two districts headed by *bada hakims* (chief administrative officers) plus three Kathmandu Valley units headed by magistrates, all appointed by the central government.

During the first decade after the 1950 revolution the regional administration remained basically unchanged except for the gradual diminution in authority and status of the *bada hakims,* whose authority under the Ranas had been virtually absolute within their jurisdictions. The powers of the *bada hakims* remained broad, but their position was weakened gradually by developments in other spheres of administration; judicial reforms, for example, deprived them of most former judicial functions.

The prestige of the *bada hakims* was also adversely affected by their inclusion within the regular civil service system at the level of departmental secretaries but ranked behind them in protocol. Efforts were made to abolish the political basis of *bada hakim* appointments by specifying that these officers were to be drawn exclusively from the ranks of the civil service. These regulations were perhaps impractical. At any rate, they were ignored in both the 1955 and 1961 reorganizations of district administration.

Other techniques, ranging from frequent transfers and dismissals to the periodic dispatch of *daudahas* (tour commissions) to the districts, were devised in the attempt to secure more effective central supervision over the *bada hakims*. These efforts were largely thwarted, in part by the inadequacy of communications and in part by the fact that few central secretariat officials had ever served in the districts or comprehended the realities of district administration.

The reorganization of districts into larger, more coherent units had long been a stated objective of the government. No progress was made in this direction, however, until King Mahendra commenced his basic reorganization of the political and administrative system following the December, 1960, coup. A particularly far-reaching reform was the division of Nepal into seventy-five development districts grouped in fourteen zones (*anchals*). The emphasis on development has brought together mountain, midland, and Terai areas within a single zone, marking a complete break with the traditional pattern under which districts were delimited within geographical areas as homogeneous as the mountainous terrain would permit. The government's objectives in making these changes were stated to be administrative uniformity and more effective implementation of development projects. Vertical zonal divisions should indeed facilitate river valley development, and the political effects of the zonal divisions may prove of importance in the nation-building process.

Commissioners were appointed to the fourteen zones and officers to the seventy-five development districts. However, the advent of zones and development districts did not immediately mean the abolition of the old district system, which for some time continued to function in only a slightly different fashion. An artificial, and essentially impractical division of functions and jurisdictions was at first contrived, under which the zonal commissioners and development district officers were primarily responsible for development programs, and the *bada hakims* for general administration. The confusion in the regional administrative system was further compounded by the presence of panchayat assemblies and executive committees at both the development district and zonal levels. These panchayats were assigned the task of assisting development programs, but were also charged with the supervision of lower-level panchayats. Superimposed upon this already complex structure were the zonal guidance officers, appointed by the Panchayat Ministry with broad supervisory powers over the entire regional administrative structure.

The lines of authority between these various officials and institutions obviously required definition. The government had stated earlier that once the panchayat and zonal systems were in sound working order the old administrative districts would be discontinued. This occurred in December, 1965, with the abolition of the office of *bada hakim*. The powers and functions of that office, however, were not transferred to the elected district panchayats, as recommended in the 1963 report of the Decentralization Commission, but to the government-appointed zonal commissioners and assistant zonal commissioners. Whether or not these powers would eventually be transferred to the district panchayats was not made clear.

The inconsistency between promise and performance is in part a reflection of the division of opinion within the government itself on the decentralization policy. According to one source,[1] the Panchayat Ministry has had a strong community development orientation and has espoused a policy directed at expanding the role of the local and district panchayats in the decision-making process on relevant questions. The predominant view in the other government departments, however, treats the panchayats as administrative units responsible for the implementation of policy decided by the central authorities. The emphasis is on administrative efficiency, and the obvious

[1] Pashupati Shamsher, "Whither Decentralization," *Vasuda* XI (July–August, 1968), pp. 13–14.

preference is for the devolution of authority to centrally-appointed district level officers rather then to panchayats.

The abolition of the old administrative district headed by a *bada hakim* in 1965 eliminated some of the institutional confusion on the regional level, but did not answer all questions on the distribution of powers among a variety of competing locally-elected and centrally-appointed officers. The basic difficulty lies in the area of conflict which persists between the objectives of a decentralized political system and the urgent need for an effective administrative structure on all levels—central, regional, and local. It is one of the paradoxes of contemporary Nepali politics that the institutions required for political decentralization cannot reasonably be expected to function effectively without the guidance and assistance of an increasingly centralized, interdependent bureaucracy. The trend toward administrative centralization is clearly dominant at present, making decentralization elsewhere in the political system that much more impractical.

Local Administration

As with other levels of administration, local government in Nepal prior to 1950 was a veritable museum of systems either inherited by the Shah conquerors or borrowed and adapted from India. Two general patterns of administration had emerged, however, one applicable in the Terai and the other in the hills and Kathmandu Valley. The names of offices and officials varied locally, but the functions performed were usually broadly similar.

The local administration in rural areas was primarily an instrument for the collection of land revenue, with assorted police and judicial functions attached. Despite repeated attempts since 1920 to reform and reorganize local government, the system continued virtually unchanged until the inauguration of Panchayat Raj in 1962. Indeed, there is reason to believe that in some areas the existing local government structure rapidly adapted to the panchayat system, and that in much of rural Nepal the new political institutions mark a change in nomenclature rather than in the power or administrative structure.

The Rana regime had, in its last years, made several attempts to introduce elected panchayat institutions at the village level and municipal councils in urban areas, but with little lasting effect. The post-revolution governments continued these efforts to reorganize the local government system. A Local Self-Government Ministry was established in 1951. Two years later a new Municipality Act was promulgated which was, however, only a slightly modified version of the 1949 Municipality Act enacted by the Rana regime. But elections were actually held in several urban areas under the 1953 Act, marking the first time that any of the local government legislation had ever been implemented to any degree.

A Village Panchayat Act was promulgated in 1956, amending and supplementing the 1949 Act. The only substantive changes, however, were the provisions specifying a population limitation for village panchayats and granting the panchayats limited powers of taxation denied them under earlier ordinances. The Nepali Congress government had piloted new panchayat legislation through the Parliament in 1960 which granted the panchayats more liberal taxation powers plus limited judicial powers. However, this bill had not received royal approval by the time of the December, 1960, coup and was never implemented.

Despite all this legislative activity, the local government policy was not a conspicuous success. A few municipal councils were functioning, more or less efficiently, but only slightly more than eight hundred village panchayats had been established by 1962, and few of these had proved to be either popular or successful from the local viewpoint.

Another Village Panchayat Act was enacted in 1961 as part of King Mahendra's program for a decentralized political system. The new law provides for the establishment of a village assembly (*gram sabha*) in each primary panchayat, consisting of all Nepali citizens over twenty-one years of age. The assembly's principal function is to elect the chairman, vice-chairman, and members of the village panchayat, which has been granted limited taxing, administrative, and judicial powers broadly similar to those projected in the Nepali Congress' village panchayat bill. The central government's ultimate authority over the village panchayats is assured by provisions granting the panchayat ministry discretionary powers to suspend or dissolve a panchayat and to appoint a provisional panchayat in its place.

A new Town (*nagar*) Panchayat Act was also enacted in 1962 to replace the 1953 Municipality Act, but here again only insignificant changes were made in the powers and functions assigned to the local government units. Indeed, the 1962 law is to some extent less liberal in that the government is granted more direct forms of control over municipalities than under the 1953 Act. The elected body under the earlier legislation has been replaced by a council in which the government nominates up to one-fourth of the members and also appoints a "local officer" to exercise broad supervisory powers over the panchayat. Moreover, the provision of the 1959 Town Panchayat Act which required the approval of the central authorities for the municipal budget has been reintroduced.

Thus, the new panchayat system does not, as yet, represent a substantial change in the local government system, at least insofar as nominal powers and functions are concerned. What is novel, however, is the vigor and speed with which these new institutions were established, in marked contrast to the record of previous governments. Nationwide elections for village and town panchayats were held in 1962 and every second year thereafter. Approximately 3,500 village panchayats and fourteen town panchayats were established, providing for the first time the basis for an integrated local government system.

It is hard to evaluate the local-level panchayats on the basis of the inconclusive and sometimes contradictory data presently available. Initial public skepticism is said to have been replaced by grudging acceptance. Local disputes and disagreements are brought before the panchayats for settlement. Competition for control of these bodies has certainly become more intense with each election since 1962. So far, the traditional elite groups of rural Nepal have usually succeeded in maintaining control over the local councils, but their dominance has not gone unchallenged. As noted in Chapter 5, the government's land reform program in the Terai has touched off several bitter disputes among the dominant elites which could not be settled locally, but required the forceful intervention of reluctant central authorities.

Some of the purposes for which the local panchayats were originally established have not been well served. At best, their contribution to economic and community development programs has been minimal; at worst, counterproductive. Local leaders pin the responsibility for failure on their own exclusion from both the formulation and implementation of policy. There are good reasons, however, for Kathmandu's view that these local bodies are not yet strong enough to bear the weight of additional responsibility. Nevertheless, the government may find it increasingly difficult to withstand the pressure for greater local autonomy in view of the repeated official acceptance of a long-range policy of political and administrative decentralization.

Judicial and Legal Systems

Extreme diversity characterized the judicial system in Nepal for nearly a century after the Gorkha conquest of Kathmandu. The Shah dynasty inherited a well-developed judicial system from the Newars of Kathmandu Valley, which supplemented their own social and legal code dating back to the regime of Ram Shah (early seventeenth century).[2] However, it was only with the advent of the Rana family system that there was any coherent endeavor to extend this legal structure to other areas of the country. In furthering the official policy of enforced Brahmanization of social behavior—introduced by King Prithvi Narayan Shah—Jang Bahadur Rana rationalized the judicial structure and codified legal principles. Political considerations made it imperative for the founder of the Rana sys-

[2] For an excellent description of the pre-Rana judicial and legal system see Brian H. Hodgson, "Some Account of the Systems of Law and Police, as Recognized in the State of Nepal," *Journal of the Royal Asiatic Society*, I (1834), 258–279.

tem to proceed cautiously, but his successors continued the task with determination. By the time of Chandra Shamsher (1901–1928), a standardized legal code and stratified judicial system had emerged.

During the later Rana period, officials such as *bada hakims,* rajas, and *mukhiyas* (whose appointments were not, properly speaking, judicial) as well as caste panchayats were given duties of a judicial character. It is difficult to fit them precisely into the court system, for essentially they functioned as mediators in disputes rather than as judges, though their decisions were often final. On the lowest level of true courts were the Amini courts in the Terai and the Adalats in the hills, sixty-nine in all. The jurisdiction of these courts was limited territorially but not by subject, since both civil and criminal cases could originate at this level. Superimposed over these courts were thirteen courts of appeal, including two appellate courts in Kathmandu. The latter were the only courts in Nepal whose jurisdiction was differentiated by category; owing to the heavy case load in Kathmandu, one of the appellate courts handled criminal cases and the other civil.

In the course of developments during the Rana regime, the old Bharadari (Council of Nobles) was stripped of nearly all political functions, but retained judicial functions as a high court hearing appeals from lower court decisions. The Bharadari is also known to have served as a court of original jurisdiction, as in the Praja Parishad conspiracy trial of 1940. When so doing, the Bharadari was expanded to include all Ranas on the role of succession as well as the most prominent non-Rana officials.

The 1856 Sanad endowed the prime minister with the

highest judicial authority in Nepal. He was, in essence, the ultimate court of appeal, and, indeed, all cases involving capital punishment or the Panchkhat crimes (five grievous sins of orthodox Hinduism) [3] were forwarded to him for final decision.

The constitutional system promulgated by Prime Minister Padma Shamsher in 1948 projected a substantial modification of the judicial system. Village panchayats were to be entrusted with jurisdiction over elementary civil and criminal cases, while Courts of First Instance (equivalent to the Amini and Adalat courts) were to have original jurisdiction over more important cases. On the next level, Courts of Appeal were projected, while the Pradhan Nyayalaya (High Court) was to be the highest court in the regular court system. In addition, the prime minister would have the power to appoint a Judicial Committee, drawn mostly from the legislature, "to act as the Supreme Court of Appeal in special cases."

Potentially, the most significant aspect of this new organic law was the way in which it affected the judicial powers of the prime minister. The constitution reserved the prime minister's right to grant pardons, reprieves, respite or remission of punishment, or to suspend, remit, or commute sentences imposed by any court, but it did not provide for his direct participation in judicial proceedings as such, a right the Rana prime ministers had utilized in political trials on several occasions. This could have guaranteed the courts greater independence in such trials,

[3] The "Panchkhat" crimes are: (1) killing a Brahman, (2) killing a cow, (3) killing a woman, (4) killing a child, and (5) Patki, or all "unlawful" intercourse of the sexes, particularly as related to the caste system.

since previously the court's decision had inevitably been the prime minister's decision.[4]

Although the 1948 Constitution was abrogated in 1951, the judicial system projected in that document has continued to exert a strong influence over later reforms of the court system. This was not immediately evident, however. The first important step toward judicial reform—the 1952 Pradhan Nyayalaya Act—bestowed on the High Court powers and status broadly approximating those of the Supreme Court of India, and thus considerably greater than those given the High Court in the 1948 Constitution. Since that date, however, there has been a steady diminution in the powers of the High Court until today it resembles far more the Pradhan Nyayalaya proposed by Padma Shamsher than the Supreme Court of India.

The first step in the downgrading of the High Court was the Royal Proclamation of 1954 which substantially amended the 1952 Act. The proclamation declared, in essence, that the crown, and not the High Court, was the highest judicial authority in Nepal. It also deprived the court of such important powers as the right, in certain cases, to issue writs of habeas corpus. The public outcry was sufficiently strong to cause the government to reinstate the Pradhan Nyayalaya in 1955 as the highest court of appeal. But the following year new legislation was enacted under which the High Court, although raised to the status of Supreme Court, actually suffered a further diminution of powers. The Supreme Court could not issue orders or

[4] During the 1940 Praja Parishad conspiracy trial, for instance, Prime Minister Juddha Shamsher participated directly in the proceedings, and reportedly intimidated the Bharadari Court into imposing more severe punishments on some of the prisoners than the court had considered justified.

decide a case as independently as had the High Court, and was given only limited consultative powers in the appointment of district court judges. Most important, however, was the article reserving the royal prerogatives with regard to the reduction or enhancement of the judicial processes and powers of the court, thus seriously undermining the independence of the Supreme Court and, indeed, of the whole judicial system.

The lower court structure was also reorganized gradually between 1956 and 1960. The Amini and Adalat courts were replaced by Ilaqa Adalats (district courts), while Zilla Adalats (regional courts) were formed as first courts of appeal. A new tier was inserted between the regional courts and the Supreme Court when three Uccha Adalats (high courts) were established to act as appellant courts and also to serve in certain cases as courts of original jurisdiction.

Once King Mahendra had thoroughly reorganized the administrative system following the December, 1960, coup, he turned his attention to the courts.[5] On November 14, 1961, an ordinance was promulgated abolishing the three Uccha Adalats, but bestowing their powers and functions on the Supreme Court. On November 15, a Supreme Court (Amendment) Act was promulgated specifying conditions under which the chief justice, permanent judges, and additional *ad hoc* judges of the Supreme

[5] The Village Panchayat Act (1961) bestowed limited judicial powers upon the village panchayats, but their exact position in the judicial structure is not yet clear. For the most part, they have been granted jurisdiction over minor civil and criminal cases, while the Zilla Adalat is still the court of original jurisdiction for any important civil or criminal case. Moreover, apparently it will be some time before village panchayats are actually allowed to utilize the judicial powers bestowed upon them by the 1961 Act.

Court were to be appointed, bringing the judicial appointment process under even firmer royal control. Four days later the regional and district court system was reorganized. By 1965 there was a Zilla Adalat in each of the 75 development districts and Anchal Adalats in each of the 14 zones.

LAW SYSTEM

Prior to 1950, the law as applied by Nepali courts was either codified law or customary law. There was no concept of "case law" (i.e., judge-made law), and previous decisions were not cited as precedents. Since the revolution, a case law system is being introduced gradually, and according to the 1962 Constitution, Supreme Court decisions must be applied by the lower courts. This system does not as yet work effectively. The lack of an organized record system and trained personnel to keep records is one obstacle. Communications between courts of various levels are poor, and lower courts are often unfamiliar with higher court decisions. Moreover, well-trained lawyers ready and able to use higher court decisions as precedents do not usually plead cases in the lower courts where their services are most needed. Reportedly, lower-court judges tend to ignore case law, and the codified law continues to play a more important role in their decisions.

Codified law in Nepal may be divided into two main categories: the *Muluki Ain* (legal code), and post-1951 legislation including the 1962 Constitution.[6] Several major

---

[6] A third form of codified law, the *Muluki Sawal* (Legal Rules) codified by Prime Minister Chandra Shamsher in 1918, was repealed in 1966. During the Rana regime the courts had accorded primacy to these regulations, and occasionally even continued to apply them after the 1950–1951 revolution.

ethnic groups had their own well-developed legal codes dating back before the Gorkha conquest, but Jang Bahadur Rana was the first ruler to consolidate them into one standardized written code, the *Muluki Ain*. The code, as it applied to social behavior, was based on the shastras of orthodox Hinduism. In general, however, the *Muluki Ain* permitted each ethnic group to follow its own local customs except for a few basic Brahmanic precepts with respect to cow-slaughter and ritual pollution and purification—a procedure guaranteed by the fact that judgeships were a virtual monopoly of Brahmans in most parts of Nepal. With these exceptions, judges usually applied local customary law. Indeed, familiarity with the customs of the various "tribes" was one of the primary qualifications for appointment to the judiciary.

The *Muluki Ain* was retained in its entirety after the 1950–1951 revolution. But while the caste provisions of the code remained applicable, they were seldom enforced except in some of the more remote rural areas. It was not until 1963 that an amended legal code was promulgated which substantially modified the *Muluki Ain*. The 1963 code specifically abolished discrimination on the basis of caste or community, and legalized inter-caste marriage, thus nullifying in theory the fundamental shastric base of the old code. In actual practice, however, the government has proceeded cautiously in implementing these controversial rules. Efforts by the Kathmandu "untouchables" to open some Hindu temples traditionally restricted to high-caste Hindus, for instance, were officially discouraged by the authorities who warned against "actions prejudicial to the social customs and traditions of others." [7] This is one more melancholy example of a tendency—observable

[7] *Gorkhapatra* (December 6, 1963).

world-wide—for official words to outrun official action in the redressing of entrenched injustices of long standing.

The other form of written law is the legislation enacted since 1951 which has not been abrogated or superseded. Here again there is no established principle with regard to conflict between legislation and other forms of codified law, and the judge has full authority to decide which type of law to apply in each case. The one exception is the 1962 Constitution, which "is the fundamental law of Nepal," and all legislation conflicting with it is "inapplicable to the extent of the conflict."

The utilization of lawyers in judicial proceedings is a post-Rana phenomenon. Lawyers have functioned at the Supreme Court level since the mid-1950's, but it has been only recently that they have become active in the lower courts, where for various reasons they have not been welcomed with any degree of enthusiasm. Judges in the lower courts, for the most part trained in the old traditional system, tend to view the presence of lawyers in their courtrooms as an irritating innovation. In many respects, the lawyers trained in modern law and the judges, who prefer to apply the old legal rules or customary law, do not even speak the same legal language. As matters now stand, the insertion of lawyers into legal proceedings has greatly increased the cost of obtaining justice without countervailing benefits in increased speed or efficiency. There is now a law college in Kathmandu, however, whose graduates number about fifty a year, and can be expected to play an increasingly important function in the Nepali legal system.

With the lack of a developed case law system, there is no substantial degree of standardization in legal decisions. In similar cases one judge might apply local customary law, another the *Muluki Ain,* and a third, post-1951 legislation; all these decisions are at present equally valid and not subject to reversal on this basis alone.

Even more serious are the limitations, both explicit and implied, upon the independence of the judiciary. The provisions under which the king can abolish any court in Nepal—a power which the present monarch has used on occasion—can affect the tenure of a judge and result in his *de facto* dismissal. The king can also reduce or enlarge the jurisdiction of any court at his own discretion. Under the 1962 Constitution, the king can dismiss a Supreme Court judge if the National Panchayat or a commission *appointed by* the king should charge that the judge "is unable to discharge the duty of his post because of lack of capacity to work or of bad conduct." Furthermore, on the recommendation of the Judicial Committee, *which he appoints,* the king can force the Supreme Court to re-examine any of its decisions. And finally, the king's broad appointive and promotion powers provide him with a powerful instrument through which the judiciary can be influenced. It is possible, given the patchwork character of the judicial system as it now exists, that for the immediate future the interests of justice are best furthered by the reservation of such sweeping crorective powers, provided they are exercised sparingly and judiciously. In the long run, a matrix such as this can scarcely be expected to foster the development of a judicial system adequate to the needs of a modern society.

4. Political Forces in Nepal

Organizations possessing the general characteristics of political parties are of recent origin in Nepal. During most of the nineteenth century, politics in Nepal was based primarily on family or communal considerations. The noble families claiming Kshatriya (warrior caste) status and the collateral lines of the royal family tended to act as integral political units, although occasionally families were divided into warring factions. An intense rivalry for administrative positions between high-caste Newari and Brahman families—engendering bitterness which has not yet subsided—was both communal and familial in nature. The broad mass of the people took little or no part in nineteenth-century Nepali politics, which was the preserve of a few small groups: the landowning nobility, Brahman priests and landowners, and the Newari commercial community. Only rarely were persons from other castes or communities entrusted with important official responsibilities, either civil or military. There were no viable intergroup institutions through which political issues could be discussed and decisions reached. As a consequence, politics was palace-oriented and largely conducted through intrigue and conspiracy. Over the years, these skills were developed to a high level of sophistication—a level which has been maintained in large measure to the present day.

In the early years of Rana rule, politics centered around conspiracies initiated by members of the royal family and the non-Rana nobility, sometimes assisted by dissident members of the Rana family. These conspiracies generally were directed toward the extinction of the dominant wing of the Rana family. By 1885, however, with the rise to power of the Shamsher wing of the Rana family, the political situation had substantially changed. By this time most of the old noble families, weakened by the severe suppression of their unsuccessful conspiracies, had made their peace with the regime. Brahman support had been gained, in part through the restoration of lands confiscated by the monarch in 1806, and in part by the ultraorthodox policies followed by the Ranas in religious and social affairs. Some Newari families had been assured important hereditary posts in the administration; others had benefited from the strict regulation imposed on foreign mercantile interests. None of these groups was completely satisfied with its position, but each had sufficient stake in the regime to deter the emergence of a united opposition. Thus, the years from 1885 to 1930, although marked by sporadic disputes within the Rana family, were outwardly quiet, and witnessed no serious challenge to the regime itself from outside the family.

During these years, the impetus toward change was inspired by developments in India and centered upon social and religious reform. Thus a branch of the Hindu reform society, the Arya Samaj, was founded in Kathmandu in 1896, receiving an enthusiastic response from sections of the Kathmandu public. But the political balance, observably delicate and further complicated by growing tensions within the Rana family itself, appeared to the rulers to be threatened by any hint of reform. By 1905 the Arya Samaj was suppressed and its founder expelled from Nepal. Later several young Samajists came under the influence of Gandhi, and a movement to popularize the *charkha* (spinning wheel) as a symbol of self-sufficiency was introduced. This movement, too, was banned. The Rana regime's unwillingness to tolerate even those movements advocating peaceful social and religious reform led to an increase in the influence of Bengali and other Indian nationalist groups advocating violent political change. Eventually some young Nepalis became convinced that terrorist tactics were the only answer to the oppressive Rana autocracy.

By the 1930's, organizations of various sorts began to emerge in Kathmandu. A secret society, the Prachanda Gorkha, formed in 1931 with the aid of Indian terrorists, plotted the destruction of the entire Rana family, but was betrayed and its members imprisoned. More cautiously, the Nepali Nagarik Adhikar Samiti (Nepali People's Rights Committee) focused upon social and religious reform, although with definite political overtones that eventually caused it to be banned. The most influential organization was the Praja Parishad, founded in 1935 by several young Kathmandu intellectuals, including Tanka Prasad Acharya. In contrast to the Prachanda Gorkha, the Praja Parishad was not conceived solely as a tight conspiratorial group limited to terrorist tactics, but also hoped to provide the nucleus for a mass anti-Rana political movement. This organization, because of the unofficial (and unacknowledged) affiliation of King Tribhuvan, became the most serious threat faced by the Rana regime in more than half a century.

There was at this time little organized anti-Rana activity among Nepalis resident in India, largely because of the close supervision maintained by British authorities, at the request of the Rana rulers. Several Nepalis nevertheless joined the Indian National Congress and received their political education in the Indian independence movement.

With the end of the second world war and the imminence of Indian independence, the anti-Rana movement entered a new phase. Both the Ranas and their opponents recognized that the regime would be seriously weakened by the British withdrawal from India. For the first time, Nepali organizations which could be called political parties made their appearance in India and shortly thereafter, on a limited scale, within Nepal. These parties had revolutionary goals, but a broader political vision than the earlier terrorist organizations. They were less concerned with the extinction of the Ranas, as such, than with the development of an alternative political force, although the distinction between these goals was not always clearly perceived.

The most important of these new political organizations was the Nepali National Congress, founded in Calcutta in January, 1947, by B. P. Koirala and other young Nepali intellectuals. The party was frankly revolutionary in its objectives, though at this time it expressed a preference for nonviolent tactics. From 1947 to 1949 a number of strikes and *satyagraha* (nonviolent resistance) campaigns were launched in various areas of Nepal. The immediate results were not impressive, but these campaigns were instrumental in crystallizing opposition to the Ranas and in fostering the impression that the days of the regime were numbered.

A second party, the Nepali Democratic Congress, was founded in 1948 by a more moderate anti-Rana group resident in India, including several former government officials who had been forced to leave Nepal. The party enjoyed less popular appeal among the Nepali residents in India than the Nepali National Congress, but it could at least count on adequate financial backing because of the affiliation of two Class C Ranas with extensive investments in India, Subarna Shamsher and Mahabir Shamsher.

The merger of these parties-in-exile into the Nepali Congress in April, 1950, brought together the two most vigorous anti-Rana forces and prepared the way for the first serious attempt to overthrow the regime. Nonviolent tactics were quietly discarded as inappropriate and it was secretly agreed that an armed insurrection was necessary and should not be long delayed.[1] Support from India was essential to the success of the venture, and the assistance of several leaders of the Indian Socialist Party as well as the ruling party, the Indian National Congress, was sought and obtained. However, Prime Minister Nehru, who apparently was not privy to all these maneuvers and counter-maneuvers, adopted a more equivocal position, since a violent revolution ran contrary to his "middle way" approach to political reform and growth in Nepal.

[1] This decision was not made public in order to avoid embarrassing the Indian government, whose sympathies were with reform, but whose central concern was with political stability along India's vulnerable northern border.

In Kathmandu Valley, meanwhile, a less overtly revolutionary anti-Rana political movement—the Nepal Praja Panchayat—had emerged in October, 1948. The Praja Panchayat planned to work through the panchayat system incorporated in the 1948 Constitution, with the intention of gradually eliminating its nondemocratic features. Relations between the Nepali Congress and the Praja Panchayat had never been close. Indeed, the leaders of both organizations viewed the other's activities with scarcely disguised suspicion. The strongly nationalist Praja Panchayat mistrusted the Indian base of the Nepali Congress and the apparent pro-India inclination of several of its leaders, while Nepali leaders in India tended to view the gradualist program of the Praja Panchayat as, in effect, a front for the Ranas. At one point, Prime Minister Mohan Shamsher did indeed appear to have considered using the Praja Panchayat for his own purposes, but the party's insistence on the implementation of the 1948 Constitution dashed any hopes he may have entertained. Instead, leaders of the party were arrested and imprisoned. With this rash move the Ranas helped seal their own doom, for the regime's last possible source of even limited popular support was thereby alienated.

The 1950 revolution, organized by the Nepali Congress, eventually obtained the support of virtually all anti-Rana political organizations with the exception of the recently organized Nepali Communist Party and the splinter wing of the Nepali National Congress led by D. R. Regmi. The Kathmandu intellectuals and the remnants of the Praja Panchayat group rallied to support the revolt once it had been launched, despite their suspicions of the Nepali Congress leadership and its Indian affiliations. They were responsible for organizing the massive demonstrations in Kathmandu that shook the foundations of Rana rule and helped deter British support of the regime in its supreme moment of crisis.

The Post-Revolution Period

Although the revolt brought the Nepali Congress to the forefront, the circumstances surrounding the February, 1951, cease-fire agreement at once exposed serious deficiencies in the organization. When a Congress commander, K. I. Singh, rejected the cease-fire agreement as a betrayal and refused to lay down arms, the new government had to confess incapacity to deal with the situation and called for Indian help. The prestige of the government was further undermined when K. I. Singh managed to escape from his prison in western Nepal, and Indian constabulary forces had to be utilized a second time to effect his recapture. He was then brought to Kathmandu where the prison facilities were presumably more secure, with even more humiliating results. Not only did his supporters rescue him in short order, but in so doing they were assisted by a unit of the Raksha Dal, the military wing of the Nepali Congress, which had been brought to Kathmandu after the revolution for the express purpose of strengthening the party's authority. During this insurrection the Congress ministers were forced into hiding, leaving it to King Tribhuvan, supported by the royal bodyguard, to prevent K. I. Singh from carrying out a successful *coup d'état*. It was thus made dramatically clear that Indian support and the participation of King Tribhuvan had been indispensable to the success of the Congress, whose intrinsic lack of strength had been laid bare.

It is not surprising that the modified form of party government introduced into Nepal by the terms of the cease-fire and buttressed by subsequent legislation (such as the Interim Government Act of 1951) ended in failure. It was not to be expected that a viable political party system could immediately emerge from the circumstances that had brought about Rana downfall. No party at that time had any broad degree of popular support or nationwide organizational structure. In the first few months of 1951, the Nepali Congress, had it been united, might well have managed to establish itself firmly throughout Nepal. The political vacuum caused by the overthrow of the Ranas had left local elites searching for a new political foundation. But having achieved victory so cheaply, the Congress leaders overlooked the fact that their success could not be attributed primarily to their own strength, and did nothing to build up a firm party structure. Instead, the party leadership rapidly became involved in personal rivalries and allowed the party to disintegrate further.

The ill-assorted cabinet established immediately after the revolution with the former Rana Prime Minister, Mohan Shamsher, at its head, could accomplish little, and rumblings of discontent were soon heard. Effective opposition stemmed from three main sources: Nepali Congress members who refused to accept the compromise agreement with the Ranas, a faction within the Rana family, and those Kathmandu political workers who had all along refused to affiliate with the Congress. This last group, many of whom had suffered imprisonment and harsh treatment under the Ranas, particularly resented the Congress refusal to share political rewards with them. Under the Ranas this Kathmandu elite had enjoyed a virtual monopoly of lower and middle echelon positions in the government, and they felt threatened by the prominence of Terai Brahman interests in the Nepali Congress. Further, the tendency of Congress leaders to run to New Delhi for guidance in every crisis did nothing to allay fears that Nepal's sovereignty might yet be compromised, and that the Nepali Congress might prove to be the instrument through which an overwhelming Indian influence on Nepal's governmental processes would be exerted.

Opposition to the Congress, however, lacked the strength to weld the political activists of Kathmandu into an effective political organization. Some did affiliate with one party or another where their intensely parochial interests often proved divisive, but the majority preferred to remain independent, seeking to attain their political objectives through narrowly based social organizations or palace politics. Their experience in the arts of intrigue, conspiracy, and character assassination sometimes proved personally advantageous, but at the expense of the growth of democratic politics or the development of a viable party system.

Rana opposition to the Congress operated for the most part behind the scenes, but the Bir Gorkha Dal (later the Gorkha Parishad) was organized in 1951 by one branch of the family. This party made its appeal to conservative, ultranationalist, religiously orthodox opinion, and more particularly to ex-servicemen who had served in British Gurkha units or the Nepal Army. The Gorkha Dal was able to organize effective opposition to the Congress, especially in some hill districts around Kathmandu Valley, but its emphasis upon a narrow "Gorkhali" nationalism deprived it of any significant influence in Kathmandu Valley, the Terai, or among the Kirati hill people of eastern Nepal.

In short, no party or coalition of parties emerged in the immediate post-revolution period which could challenge the Congress. The chief threat to the Congress arose not from the opposition but from the dissension within its own ranks, particularly from the power struggle between the half brothers M. P. and B. P. Koirala. When the Nepali Congress ministers forced the resignation of Mohan Shamsher in November, 1951, it had been assumed that Home Minister B. P. Koirala would be named prime minister. Instead, King Tribhuvan appointed the party's president, M. P. Koirala. The intense maneuvering which followed eventually forced M. P. Koirala from the party presidency and not long thereafter (August, 1952) from the cabinet as well, but not before the tactics used had brought the party into disrepute.

M. P. Koirala later (April, 1953) founded his own political organization, the Rashtriya Praja (National Democratic) Party, taking much of the Kathmandu branch of the Congress with him. This split was the most conspicuous but by no means the only serious division in the ranks of the Nepali Congress. Two other minor wings of the party had already broken away in protest. One Terai-based faction, led by Bhadrakali Mishra, later organized the Jana (People's) Congress, while the "Banarsi Brahmans," under Balchandra Sharma, founded the Nepali Congress Progressive Group.

By 1954, the party system had sunk into chaos and confusion. What remained of the Nepali Congress was still disunited. Party workers were disheartened both by the ease with which the Congress had been forced out of power and by the failure of all attempts to regain office. Only the combined efforts of such leaders as B. P. Koirala, Subarna Shamsher, Ganeshman Singh, and Surya Prasad Upadhyaya saved the party from dissolution.

Yet no other party or coalition of parties had emerged to supplant the Nepali Congress. The experiences of the first and second M. P. Koirala governments had demonstrated that the road to office lay not through popular support but through royal favor. This realization diminished any interest party leaders might have had in building up their organizations. The familiar game of palace intrigue and "bazaar-rumor politics" appeared to be the most fruitful channel for the attainment of political goals. As the prospect of general elections receded into the dim future, it became easy to fall back on wild but unverifiable claims to popular support.

Moreover, the disintegrative process that had undermined the Nepali Congress had afflicted the other parties as well. After an initial organizing phase in 1951, the various parties had rapidly fallen apart into mutually recriminative personal factions. Concepts of party responsibility or party loyalty were virtually nonexistent. Parties split, regrouped in new coalitions no less volatile than their predecessors, and shortly thereafter split again. Most party leaders, intent upon obtaining ministerial posts, were quite prepared to advance their personal ambitions at the expense of party solidarity.

Of the numerous political parties organized in the 1947–1954 period, only three—the Nepali Congress, the Communist Party, and the Gorkha Parishad—could possibly qualify as "national" parties on the basis of the social and regional origins of their core leadership groups.[2] The remainder were largely clustered about a single personality and committed to narrowly defined personal interests. By and large, the rank and file of the parties came from either Kathmandu Valley or the Terai, the two regions which most immediately felt the impact of the 1951 revolution, as well as having more town dwellers, a higher education level, and a larger student population. With the exception of the Communists, the parties recruited members openly and freely with little concern for ideological predilections or personal motivations. Typically, a party member's loyalty was to a leader rather than to an organization, and he was ready to move from one party or group to another at the leader's behest. Party cohesiveness was further weakened by the inadequacy of transportation and communication facilities which prevented the party headquarters in Kathmandu from exercising effective control over local party branches.

In assessing the first four years of "democracy," Mahendra, then Crown Prince, declared:

But it is a matter of great shame that we cannot even point to four important achievements we have made during this period. If we say that democracy is still in its infancy, we have seen such qualities as selfishness, greed, and jealousy, which are not to be found in an infant. And if we say that it has matured, unfortunately we do not see it flourishing anywhere.[3]

[2] See the analysis of B. L. Joshi and L. E. Rose, *op. cit.*, pp. 501–503.

[3] "Message from His Royal Highness, the Crown Prince, on National Day (February 18, 1955)," *Nepal Gazette*, Vol. IV, Extraordinary Issue, February 18, 1955.

As an appraisal of the period from 1951 to 1955, this statement not only possessed considerable validity, but also represented the prevailing popular viewpoint in the country. It could also be taken as a portent of future developments, for it gave expression to the distaste with which Mahendra viewed Nepal's experience with parties and government by party.

The Parties and King Mahendra

The most significant political party development in the period between King Mahendra's succession in 1955 and the general elections of 1959 was the remarkable revitalization of the Nepali Congress under the leadership of B. P. Koirala and Subarna Shamsher. One of the more important factors underlying this development was the very fact of the repeated failure of the Congress, after the resignation of the first M. P. Koirala cabinet, to attain office through royal favor. Party leaders finally came to realize that prospects of success under Mahendra were even bleaker. Dissatisfied with the system under which ministerial appointments were made, the Congress leaders decided to so broaden the base of the party that its claim to office could not be ignored.

By 1955 the strictly opportunist elements had long since left the Nepali Congress. The hard core of party workers, reinforced by younger, often ideologically oriented recruits attracted by the party's broadly socialist philosophy, provided a more solid foundation for a well-organized, disciplined party structure. The decision to utilize nonviolent direct action techniques to attain limited and popular political and economic objectives not only con-

tributed to internal discipline, but also attracted many enthusiastic young Nepalis.

Between 1956 and 1959, the Nepali Congress established branches in every district in Nepal with, for the
most part, little or no competition from other political
parties. The most serious rivals were local leaders, run-
ning as independents, although many of these found it
more advantageous to join than to oppose the party. With
the exception of the Communist Party, which managed to
organize strong units here and there in the hills and the
Terai, and the Gorkha Parishad, whose activities were
largely restricted to the hill districts immediately surrounding Kathmandu, the other parties preferred to base
their future on palace politics. It was therefore to be expected that the Nepali Congress would outdistance all
other parties in the 1959 elections. What was surprising
was the extent of its victory over independent candidates
as well.

The 1959 general elections and subsequent developments dispelled much of the uncertainty and confusion
that had surrounded party claims to popular support.
Most opposition parties had been exposed as a conglomeration of self-proclaimed leaders with little or no popular
following. These party leaders, however, failed to inter-
pret the verdict of the electorate as a warning to revamp
their approach to political tactics and work to expand and
strengthen their party structure. With few exceptions, they
continued to demonstrate a preference for the familiar
world of palace politics, even within the restricted arena
possible under a parliamentary system. The result was a
forced dependence upon the King, accompanied by a per-

ceptible muting of their erstwhile enthusiasm for parliamentary institutions.

The Nepali Congress, in contrast, looked forward confidently to a long period of tenure in office. It was a natural assumption that the advantages derived from its position as governing party, together with the absence of any genuine rival, would ensure an even more sweeping victory for the party in the second general elections, scheduled for 1964. The party leaders accepted as their model the prevailing "dominant party" system in India, fully expecting the Nepali Congress to assume the same guiding role in Nepal that the Indian Congress Party had long played under Nehru's leadership. Meanwhile, in the fall of 1960, the cabinet moved to further strengthen the already dominant position of the Nepali Congress by appointing party workers as district development officers, thus associating economic development programs intimately with the party. But soon thereafter—most unexpectedly—the B. P. Koirala government was dismissed by the King and the party itself was outlawed.

King Mahendra's motives in this drastic action have been variously interpreted, and not always charitably. He must in reality have been impelled by a variety of considerations. He could not have been unaware of the many implications of the appointment of party workers as development officers. What would be the results of the potential for corruption inherent in such an arrangement? Would the further politicization of the rural districts leave them prey to the partisan acrimony that had earlier paralyzed the capital? Would crown functions be usurped by the present prime minister and the monarch relegated to a figurehead, as had occurred under Rana prime ministers a century ago? Was the very existence of the monarchy imperiled by the growing power of the Nepali Congress, with its democratic-socialist philosophy? Was Nepal itself in danger of becoming an Indian satellite? Questions such as these may or may not have had much bearing on the actual intentions of B. P. Koirala and the Nepali Congress. Nevertheless, it would have been strange indeed if they had not arisen in the mind of a monarch who was only too aware of the underlying factors in both the founding and the collapse of the Rana regime, whose virtual prisoner he had himself once been. There is room for argument as to whether the King or the Prime Minister had charted the better course for Nepal. There can be no doubt that the failure of the King and his minister to achieve a *modus vivendi* had spelled the doom of a parliamentary experiment which had appeared to hold out a promise for substantial political stability in a much troubled land.

Whatever King Mahendra's motives may have been on December 15, 1960, his actions were dramatic, decisive, and smoothly executed. Prime Minister B. P. Koirala was arrested while addressing a youth conference, and most of his other colleagues were apprehended shortly thereafter. Only Subarna Shamsher, who had flown to Calcutta two days earlier, and two ministers who were on tour abroad, escaped arrest and imprisonment. Most opposition party leaders in Kathmandu were also arrested although, with a few exceptions, they were released shortly thereafter on signing statements supporting the King's action.

What King Mahendra had in mind was for a time unclear. At one point he appeared to be seeking a realignment of political forces within the Parliament. He did not long pursue this approach, and it is possible that he was forced into more drastic action than he had at first contemplated. In any event, on December 26, 1960, he appointed a new nonparty government, composed of independents and a few Nepali Congressmen who disassociated themselves from the party leadership. A royal proclamation was issued banning all political activity. Parties were ordered to disband, and their headquarters were closed. Shortly thereafter, the King announced that the new political system would take the form of a "partyless panchayat democracy."

The new government undertook vigorous action to enforce the ban on parties. Particular attention was paid to the Nepali Congress Party workers, in the rural districts as well as in Kathmandu, who were forced to choose between imprisonment and signing statements supporting the King and promising to refrain from political activity. Many fled to India, but many more submitted. The remaining parties, with one exception, were easily brought under control since they consisted of little more than Kathmandu headquarters with personal ties to a few party workers in the districts. The exception was the Communist Party (CPN), which had a tightly established organizational structure in several areas. The CPN went underground, but not very deeply, since the royal regime did not harass the Communists as vigorously as the Nepali Congress.

Most opposition party leaders interpreted King Mahendra's dismissal of the B. P. Koirala cabinet as favorable to their own ambitions and loudly applauded his action. Any expectations they might have had as to the improvement of their own political prospects have nevertheless remained largely unfulfilled. In the various reshuffling of cabinets since December, 1960, these political leaders have been virtually ignored, except for a few younger party members who had only tenuous party ties. Attempts by the older party leaders to improve their political bargaining power through the proposed establishment of a "national" organization inclusive of all political elements except "anti-national" rebels (i.e., the Nepali Congress), have proved unavailing because of the government's refusal to countenance any form of political organization outside the panchayat and class organization systems. Deprived of any real scope for maneuver, these former leaders had either to retire from politics or choose between continued support to the royal regime (on the King's terms) or merger with dissident forces led by the Nepali Congress.

Thus, in the present situation, only the Nepali Congress and the Communists have shown any potential for future development. The resilience displayed by the Congress following the December, 1960, coup was testimony to its intrinsic strength. The task of rebuilding the party's structure was initiated by the leaders in exile in India, but before many months an underground organization was operating in various parts of Nepal as well. The situation became in some respects reminiscent of the 1947–1950 period: once again, opposition leaders resident in India prepared the ground for a major struggle within Nepal.

The Nepali Congress, as spearhead of the opposition, was further augmented by the adherence of several leaders from other parties, including the Bharat Shamsher wing of the Gorkha Parishad. By the fall of 1961, the Congress felt sufficiently strong to launch a campaign of terrorism and sabotage, designed to obtain political concessions from King Mahendra. This campaign continued for more than a year with varying degrees of success, but was called off in December, 1962, in the wake of the Sino-Indian border war.

In retrospect, the decision to launch a limited resistance campaign against the royal regime can be seen to have been a serious miscalculation. King Mahendra, rather than weakening under pressure, hardened his attitude toward the Congress. Moreover, the manner in which political refugees guided the struggle from India antagonized many Nepali nationalists who, while not staunch adherents of the royal regime, liked the prospects of an Indian-dominated government even less. The sudden termination of the struggle in December, 1962, left the Nepali Congress in considerable disarray. Some discouraged party workers made their peace with the King; those who remained in India became comparatively inactive.

Paradoxically, the party could regain a prominent role in Nepali politics only on King Mahendra's terms—that is, by agreeing to work on an individual basis in the "partyless" panchayat system. This was a bitter pill to swallow, and it was not finally accomplished until early in 1968. In a statement issued in Calcutta—reportedly on Indian advice—by Subarna Shamsher, the Congress organization in exile in India accepted the King's terms. Several months later this led to the release of B. P. Koirala and a royal pardon for Subarna Shamsher and many of his associates. Redefining their political roles within the existing political structure has proved to be a difficult problem for Nepali Congress leaders and workers alike, but their return has been the most significant event in Nepali politics since their abrupt dismissal nearly eight years earlier.

The Communist Party has been less seriously hampered than was the Nepali Congress by the need to function underground. Party meetings and conferences are held within Nepal; party statements are freely circulated, and journals reflecting the views of factions in the party are regularly published. But if government repression has been a relatively minor problem, internal dissension has assumed major proportions.

The main issue in dispute is one that has disrupted the Communist organization since its legalization in 1956—namely, party policy toward the monarchy and, more specifically, toward King Mahendra's concept of the crown. The "moderates," such as Keshar Jang Rayamajhi and Shailendra Kumar Upadhyaya, have argued that at this stage Communists should support the existing structure—whether parliamentary, Panchayat Raj, or absolute monarchy—and work from within to establish the conditions under which Communists could come to power in the future. An "extremist" faction, led by Pushpa Lal Shrestha and Tulsi Lal Amatya, argued that the abolition of the monarchy is the only policy consistent with Communist principles, and that the party should therefore take a firm position against the present regime and help organize a revolutionary movement aimed at its overthrow, even in conjunction with such "bourgeois" political groups as the Nepali Congress.

Several attempts to reconcile these viewpoints were made during 1961, culminating in November in a "secret" plenary session of the Central Committee in Kathmandu. Far from resolving the disagreement, these sessions tended to accentuate the differences between the factions. The moderates, with a substantial majority on the Central

Committee, threatened to expel the extremists if they did not cease their "antiparty activities." Shortly thereafter, Pushpa Lal fled to India with several colleagues, subsequently proposing an alliance with the Nepali Congress rebels.

A final split in the Communist Party was avoided until mid-1962 when the faction led by Pushpa Lal summoned its supporters to a general conference. Resolutions were adopted calling for the overthrow of the royal regime and suspending ten moderate members of the Central Committee from the party for various periods on the grounds that they had supported the King's "antidemocratic" measures. The moderates countered a few days later with a statement condemning "violent actions." In September, 1962, the Rayamajhi-dominated Central Committee expelled Pushpa Lal and two other colleagues.

The "royalist" wing of the Communist Party managed to retain control over the party machinery at the center but was less successful at the district level. The support extended to the royal regime brought the Rayamajhi faction some tangible rewards, including appointments to high government posts and the opportunity to function only slightly below the legal level in their efforts to infiltrate the panchayat institutions and the secretariat. But Rayamajhi's gradualist approach had little appeal to the rank and file of the party or to pro-Communist elements among the students, who tended to favor the flamboyant program then espoused by Pushpa Lal Shrestha and Tulsi Lal Amatya from their safe exile in India. The separate identity of the various wings of the party has been maintained, although there have been reports of cooperation between them during elections to the panchayat and class organizations since 1966. The release in 1969 of Manmohan Adhikari, probably the only Nepali Communist leader with sufficient stature to gain the support of all party factions, may yet provide the stimulus for reuniting and revitalizing the party. But, as with the Nepali Congress, this has had to be based on a public, if only nominal, acceptance of King Mahendra's political objectives. Open opposition would only invite renewed suppression, and the Communists can ill afford to operate underground now that the Nepali Congress leaders, their principal rivals, are again active on the political scene.

There is little likelihood that political parties will be allowed to function openly as such in the near future, in view of the 1967 constitutional amendment specifically banning political organizations or associations and formally describing the political system as a "partyless democratic panchayat system." For while parties could be fitted into the panchayat system, as shown by the experience with similar institutions of both India and Pakistan, King Mahendra's opposition is clear-cut. He has repeatedly characterized parties as corrupt and divisive, and has accused them of being pawns of foreign powers. His insistence that former party leaders and workers can participate in panchayat politics only as individuals is based on his conviction that partisan spirit is wholly incompatible with panchayat-based democracy and national integration.

King Mahendra's strong prejudice against parties and his distrust of them as agents of modernization and political change are not without substance. The record of political parties in Nepal, as in much of the non-Western world, does not inspire confidence in their capacity to provide the leadership and authority necessary in a difficult transitional period. But the King's criticisms are more appropriately directed at a political system characterized by a multiplicity of weak parties than at a well-developed party system marked by a high degree of functional institutionalization and broad popular participation. Nor can the King escape some share of the blame for the failure of the Nepali parties to mature, for the involvement of the crown is an essential ingredient in palace politics. Furthermore, the royal coup of December, 1960, was directed against a government based upon a party that was beginning to assert both the will and the capacity to govern on its own strength. Whether or not this strength would have proved equal to the task is a matter for conjecture. If not, the King's action saved the party from becoming associated with failure and, in retrospect, has probably added to its prestige. The timing of his coup also increased his vulnerability to the charge, heard in some quarters, that a major cause of his displeasure was that the Nepali Congress was rapidly becoming an alternative to the monarch as the linchpin of the political system. In any event, the ban on political parties has not solved King Mahendra's problems. Suitable substitutes have not been created to channel the participation of newly-mobilized groups into the political system in a nondisruptive fashion, as will be seen in the discussion of nonparty political organizations which follows.

Nonparty Political Organizations

As has been noted above, a number of social and religious organizations were established during the Rana period, but for the most part their existence was brief, and their influence negligible. Nevertheless, the experience gained and the attitudes developed during that period did affect the nature of political participation after the introduction of democracy in 1951. Literally dozens of voluntary organizations were founded, some espousing social reform, educational expansion, and economic reorganization, while others aimed at protecting group interests. A comprehensive institutional structure was created, representing virtually every major component of Nepali society. Indeed, the tendency was toward overorganization, since several organizations frequently competed for the support of the same group. As might be expected, few of these organizations obtained substantial popular support. Many were highly personal, the creation of a small clique intent primarily upon receiving official recognition and its attendant benefits.

With a few notable exceptions, such as the Nepal Karmavir Mahamandal, most of the "voluntary" organizations abjured a direct interest in politics, but nevertheless they did occasionally indulge in what were essentially political activities. The 1951 united front between the Communists and Praja Parishad, for example, included a number of ostensibly nonpolitical social organizations, largely leftist in orientation. In 1955, over one hundred social and educational organizations participated in a political conference at the invitation of King Mahendra. Two years later, one of the most influential social organizations in Kathmandu Valley, the Shanti Raksha Swayam Sevak Kendra (Central Organization of Volunteers for the Preservation of Peace) organized a general strike against the government's food policy that helped force the resignation of the Tanka Prasad cabinet.

Thus the line between political and nonpolitical activity was never clearly drawn. Indeed, social and economic organizations were frequently affiliated with political parties, usually either the Nepali Congress or the Communist Party. The most important organizations among students, women, peasants, and labor had either affiliated with one of these two parties, or had been split into rival factions along party lines. The only labor union of any significance (the mill workers union in Biratnagar) was divided into pro-Congress and pro-Communist factions, of which the former was usually more influential. On the other hand, the most effective peasant organization (the Kisan Sangh) was Communist dominated. After coming to power in 1959, the Nepali Congress began to organize its own peasant's union, but the December coup terminated this drive before any real rival to the Kisan Sangh had been organized.

It was not at first clear whether the 1960 ban on political organizations also applied to voluntary organizations and to the "nonpolitical" affiliates of the parties. Official policy was clarified in March, 1961, with the announcement that six government-sponsored class and professional organizations for peasants, labor, students,[4] youth, children, and women were to be established. Later, the Ex-Servicemen's Association was added to the list. Nonofficial parallel bodies were forbidden, thus forcing most of the voluntary organizations to disband. There is reason to believe that the leadership of many organizations merely transferred to the official bodies, as is known to be true of

[4] In 1967, the National Student Organization was disbanded and each educational institution was again permitted to establish its own student organization.

student organization committees. Cadres of the Kisan Sangh are reported to have infiltrated the peasant organization, while retaining underground the structure of their own organization. The dissensions and disputes that had previously disrupted voluntary organizations have not disappeared, but are now being conducted within a different framework and under government supervision.

The class and professional organizations have a fourtier structure, directly paralleling the panchayat system. Primary (local) committees in the villages and towns are elected by all eligible members within the jurisdiction of the panchayat. Each primary unit delegates one member to a district council, which elects a five-man district executive committee. All the district committees in a zone then elect the zonal committee. The president and fourteen of the members of the central committee (one from each zone) are elected by a national congress of the organizations composed of members of the district and zonal committees. Two additional members are nominated by the president, while the secretary and treasurer are appointed by the Panchayat Ministry. The fifteen representatives of the class and professional organizations in the National Panchayat are elected by the zonal committees.

Official pronouncements on the purposes and functions of these organizations, although profuse, have seldom been specific. There was an evident intent in the early stages to use them to rechannel and diffuse the political energies which had formerly found an outlet in the parties. They were expected to serve as a more direct form of contact with popular sentiment than the panchayats could possibly provide. The government also hoped to use these bodies as vehicles for the mobilization of "voluntary labor" in support of projects for economic development and other nation-building activities.

In all these respects, the class and professional organizations have been a distinct disappointment. Nevertheless, they are the only form of political activity open to many Nepalis. From the first, aspirants for election to the National Panchayat found them useful and Communists considered them worthy of infiltration. After January, 1967, when a constitutional amendment made membership in a class or professional organization one of the qualifications for membership in the National Panchayat, a number of old-line leaders applied for membership, occasionally under rather ludicrous circumstances. But until these organizations can show signs of serving a useful purpose for the groups they nominally represent, their popularity is unlikely to grow. The government has promised that these bodies will eventually be granted broader autonomy and greater influence, but this could not be accomplished without a basic change of direction in the development of political institutions in Nepal.

It would seem that change of some sort will almost certainly occur. Modernization inevitably involves some degree of broadening of participation in the political life of a country, whether in the highly organized and stratified sense in Communist and other one-party authoritarian states or more diffusely as in democratic polities. Regimes which resist this trend do so at high cost to their rate of modernization and perhaps even to their viability. King Mahendra has not been unaware of the inadequacy of his own political system in this respect and has tried to encourage broad participation to the greatest extent possible within the system. However, the panchayats and the class and professional organizations are woefully inadequate substitutes for the political parties as two-way channels between government and the governed. Nor are they, by way of compensation for this loss of effectiveness, less of a potential threat to national unity and integration. Under a parliamentary system, after all, parties have to seek broadly based support on a national scale for any real hope of success in the competition for political power. King Mahendra's denunciations of parties as divisive and representative of "narrow, antinational" interests would apply with even greater force to the class and professional organizations if they were ever to function freely and effectively. Certainly the latter bodies have a far narrower base and a more clearly factional, if not "antinational" character. It is one of the paradoxes of Panchayat Raj that these organizations can carry out the important responsibilities assigned to them only if they assume some of the very characteristics of the party system they were created to replace.

5. The Modernization of the Nepali Economy

The isolation policy pursued so assiduously by Nepal's rulers prior to 1947 may have protected the country's political independence, but it also impeded any serious effort to modernize and reorganize the Nepali economy. The post-revolutionary governments inherited an economic structure that was in basic respects little different from that extant two centuries earlier. The changes that had occurred, such as a substantial increase in population and the progressive concentration of land ownership, had indeed lowered general living standards, at least outside Kathmandu.

Post-1951 governments in Nepal have made rapid economic development a primary goal. Positive achievements, however, have been below expectations. Some of the reasons for this—ministerial instability, administrative inadequacies, and the lack of records and statistics—are obvious and probably unavoidable. Serious misconceptions concerning the dynamics of economic development, however, would seem to have been no less critical. The tendency often has been to accept textbook principles of economic development, and then formulate impressive sounding programs on paper without a thorough investigation of their suitability to objective conditions in Nepal. A good example of this approach is the compulsory savings program which was introduced in 1964 with so little consideration of the probable consequences that it had to be suspended in 1969.

A further complication has been the policy adopted in 1955 of seeking the maximum diversification of the sources of external support for Nepal's economic development. This was intended primarily to reduce Nepal's heavy dependence upon India. The policy has some notable successes to its credit, but a high price has been paid. The exploitation of the power and water resources of the Karnali River basin in western Nepal, for instance, has probably been delayed for a decade while Kathmandu has engaged in a futile attempt to find alternative sources of foreign assistance for this project. It is questionable whether diversification has diminished Nepal's dependence upon India to any significant extent. Even now, some fifteen years after the introduction of this policy, Nepal is continually forced to make adjustments arising from an unavoidable exposure to the severe economic problems that have plagued its neighbor in recent years.[1] This has

[1] Nepal made a valiant but premature declaration of economic independence in 1966 when it refused to follow India in devaluing the rupee. It soon became clear that Kathmandu had been motivated more by emotional and political considerations than by rational economic calculations. In one stroke, the value of Indian and American foreign aid (most of the latter also comes in the form of Indian rupees from the large U.S. wheat loan holdings in that currency) was reduced by perhaps forty per cent with critical effect upon the development budget. The trade structure between India and Nepal was also thrown into disarray. The price of imported commodities rose rapidly while Nepali producers found it more difficult to compete on the Indian and world market. Nepal thus suffered all the disad-

been a hard lesson for the Nepalis to absorb psychologically, but it is nevertheless fundamental to sound economic planning.

Agrarian Policy

According to the 1961 Nepal census estimates, 97.1 per cent of the population live in settlements of less than five thousand inhabitants, and nearly nine out of ten are directly dependent upon the land. This extreme rural-urban ratio dramatizes the importance of agriculture and, in particular, of the efforts to modernize the agrarian system.

Landlord-tenant relationships are the rule in most areas, and available evidence indicates a trend toward greater concentration of land ownership in the hands of noncultivators. Such a situation under a different set of conditions could have led to large-scale operations or investment in the land, but this has not yet happened. Tenants are usually obligated to bear the costs of cultivation and assume the risks. As a result, the unit of cultivation tends to be very small—at times bordering on the marginal —and chronic depression is the lot of many cultivators. It is primarily for this reason that such large numbers of Nepalis—perhaps three million—are now residents of India and other neighboring Asian states, and have enlisted in large numbers in the British and Indian armies.

The Gorkha dynasty inherited a multitude of land tenure systems from the numerous principalities incorporated

---

vantages of devaluation but gained none of the advantages. Fortunately, the British devaluation of the pound in 1967 provided Kathmandu with the opportunity to revise its monetary policy on reasonable economic terms with no serious loss of political prestige or public confidence.

into Nepal in the eighteenth century. Most of these were retained in outwardly identical form, but were remolded by the Shah rulers to serve their own purpose. Eventually, four major types of land tenure emerged, though the variations within each category were considerable: (1) *raikar tenure:* land on which revenue was paid directly to the state, and in which the state acted the role of landowner; (2) *birta tenure:* a form of tenure, often tax-exempt, in which the state divested itself of ownership rights in favor of an individual, but usually on conditional terms; (3) *guthi tenure:* land donated by the state or by individuals for religious or philanthropic purposes, also usually tax exempt; and (4) *kipat tenure:* a form of communal land tenure, especially prevalent in the eastern hill areas.

These tenure systems were based upon the traditional theory that all lands belong to the State, a legal fiction that is maintained even today. In fact, most of the characteristics of a private ownership system exist in Nepal, even on *raikar* lands.

A number of attempts were made to rationalize the agrarian system prior to 1951. Several land surveys were conducted, but although land boundaries were redrawn, the basic characteristics of the existing tenure systems were not affected. The primary objective of the government in conducting these surveys had been to maximize land revenue and to encourage the settlement of uncultivated land. There was no interest in modernizing agrarian production or reorganizing the land ownership system. Indeed, the very concept of land reform was considered subversive by the Ranas; any efforts in this direction had to await the overthrow of the regime.

Prior to 1963, post-revolution land legislation was restricted to three subjects: reform of the chaotic tenure system, rent control, and protection of tenants against eviction. The question of tenure reform centered mainly around the abolition of the *birta* (land grant) system which was not only the most widespread form of land tenure (an estimated 28 per cent of all cultivable land) but also the one most subject to abuse. The decision to abolish *birtas* was announced in September, 1951, by the first post-revolution government, but for several years no progress was made. Not only was *birta* tenure complex, but detailed and reliable records of these holdings were lacking, as many *birta* holders refused, usually with impunity, to submit reports as ordered on several occasions by the government.

It was only in 1959, when the first elected cabinet assumed office, that a government finally found itself in a position to proceed with *birta* abolition. Under the legislation, the lands of the larger *birta* holders were nationalized (with compensation), while the comparatively small holdings were retained by their owners subject to the payment of the land revenue rate in effect on adjoining *raikar* land. After some initial hesitation, the regime that replaced the Nepali Congress cabinet in December, 1960, retained and even strengthened this program for the abolition of the *birta* system. The purpose of this program, as can be seen, was fiscal reform and the expansion of the sources of land revenue. The *birta* program has had no effect on other agrarian reform objectives such as security of tenure for tenants or redistribution of land among the large class of landless laborers.[2]

[2] See Mahesh C. Regmi, *Land Tenure and Taxation in Nepal*, Vol. II, Research Series, No. 4, Institute of International Studies (Berkeley: University of California, 1964).

An important limitation on the scope of land tenure reform is the extreme care with which the government has approached the *kipat* and *guthi* tenure systems. Important groups in often turbulent eastern Nepal—largely Limbu tribesmen—have long-standing rights under the *kipat* system, while the religious and philanthropic character of *guthi* tenure has placed these lands beyond the reach of the reformer. The royal regime is publicly committed to the retention of these land tenure systems with only minor modifications. Reforms have so far been restricted to a slight increase in land revenue assessment on *kipat* land and the regulation and standardization of *guthi* endowments.[3]

The attempt to regulate rent paid by tenant cultivators to landowners has a longer history in Nepal than tenure reform. The first rent control regulations were introduced as early as 1907 by the Rana Prime Minister Chandra Shamsher. But these had too many loopholes and escape clauses to be enforceable and had almost no effect on rental practices.

The record since the 1950 revolution has not been much improved. Limitation of land rents was proclaimed as a basic objective of the first post-revolutionary government, but it was six years before any legislation was enacted. The 1957 Lands Act fixed the maximum rent at either one-half the gross produce or the previous rent, whichever was lower, and also barred additional impositions. In effect, this only gave formal recognition to the custom, prevalent in many areas, of an equal division of the produce between the tenant cultivator and the landowner. Indeed, in some respects the new law may have

[3] *Ibid.*, Vols. III and IV.

added to the tenants' burden: it did not specify, for instance, that only the main crop was to be shared, as had been the common practice previously. Subsequent governments have considered reducing land rents to 25 per cent of production, but this reform proposal has foundered in the face of the determined opposition of powerful landlords and their allies. With the possible exception of Kathmandu Valley, where the movement for reform is better organized and capable of applying direct pressure on the Central Secretariat, it is still the normal practice for crops to be divided equally between the tenant cultivator and the landowner.

Attempts to guarantee tenancy rights to landless cultivators have as yet fared no better. Under the Rana system, tenants could be evicted at will by the landowner. A bill, drafted in 1952 by the first M. P. Koirala government, to give tenants permanent rights on land they had cultivated since 1950, was never enacted. In 1955, a royal proclamation was issued, declaring that tenants who had cultivated land for two years should be given tenancy rights and should not be evicted so long as their rents were paid. This proclamation, however, was a declaration of principle only, lacking the force of law.

An attempt was made in the Land and Cultivator's Compilation Act (1956) to provide the land-use records without which legislation guaranteeing tenant security could not be enforced. This act called for the establishment of village committees to compile up-to-date lists of tenancy occupancies. But few such committees were established, and no progress was made in compiling records. The 1957 Lands Act required local officials to maintain a list of "protected tenants" who had cultivated a plot of land for one year, and could not be evicted so long as their rent was paid. This act also made tenancy rights heritable, and, as amended in 1959, even saleable without the consent of the landowner.

This legislation did little to advance or even protect the existing rights of tenants. On the contrary, the enactment of legislation guaranteeing tenancy rights was accompanied in many areas by the wholesale eviction of tenants, many of whom had been long established cultivators on their plots of land. The 1963 Agricultural (New Arrangements) Act repeated the provisions of the earlier legislation on rent limitations and tenancy rights, but with the same initial disruptive effects. While a large number of tenancy certificates, nominally guaranteeing tenants the right to use lands which they have cultivated over an established period, have been issued under this reform program, reports indicate that the certificates are as yet of little or no value in many parts of the country.

The 1963 Act also incorporated a radical new feature in land legislation in Nepal: the placing of a ceiling on the size of landholdings.[4] The surplus lands acquired by the government were to be redistributed, with priority on

---

[4] The ceilings imposed under the 1963 Act, as amended in 1964, are: Terai and Inner Terai—25 bighas (40 acres); Kathmandu Valley—50 ropanis (6.5 acres); hill areas—80 ropanis (10.4 acres). Ceilings have also been placed on the amount of land a tenant may cultivate: 4 bighas (6.4 acres) in the Terai and Inner Terai; 10 ropanis (1.3 acres) in Kathmandu Valley; and 20 ropanis (2.6 acres) in the hills. The comparatively high ceilings in the Terai and Inner Terai are justified on the grounds that efficient large-scale farming is possible in these areas and should be encouraged, and by the fact that there are still large areas of wasteland available in some lowland districts that could be brought under cultivation.

purchase to be given first to tenants already using the land and then to landless laborers. A 1964 amendment of the 1963 Act provided for a survey of landholdings in Nepal to bring them within the ceiling limitations. By 1968 the survey had been completed and the results were extremely disheartening. In the whole of Nepal, less than 200,000 acres were declared to be surplus, and much of this was either uncultivable or was reserved forest land protected by legislation. Furthermore, virtually the entire surplus is located in the Terai lowlands where the inhabitants of the congested hill areas are still reluctant to settle. As a result, by 1969 only about half of the declared surplus lands had actually been acquired by the government and less than half of that had been redistributed. The impact on the land-hungry hill areas has been minimal, and there is no reason to expect better results in the future, given the limited quantity of surplus land available.

The 1963 land reform legislation, as amended in 1964, also included two other innovational features: the "interception" of agricultural debts by local committees which collected the debts at ten per cent interest and repaid them to the money lenders with five per cent interest; and a compulsory savings system under which cultivators, whether tenants or landowners, are required to deposit a certain percentage of their earnings or production with the local committee as a "savings" which is to be repaid after five years. The elimination of the typically usurious traditional credit system and its replacement by cooperative credit institutions were the primary objectives of these two programs. Progress in this direction has been slow, however, and most small farmers are still dependent upon the traditional money-lending class for the credit essential to the cultivation of their fields.

One thing is clear: the implementation of land reform legislation will have to await a major change in the character of the local administrative system. The panchayats may eventually provide the foundation required. Reports of the village and district panchayat elections, however, indicate that local elites, mostly landlords, control these institutions at present. Vigorous implementation of land reform legislation by these institutions should not be expected under the circumstances, even if "guided" and coerced by the land reform officers appointed under the land reform program. But the panchayat has the potential of becoming an arena in which local conflict can be conducted and eventually resolved, rather than merely repressed. Only if this potential approaches fulfillment can the local administrative system cease to be an obstacle and become an agency of reform.

Industrial Policy

The beginnings of a modern industrial complex in Nepal date only from the period of the second world war, and progress has not been substantial. Indeed, it is probable that a greater proportion of Nepal's population was employed in nonagricultural activities two centuries ago than today. An extensive homespun cotton textile industry was then able not only to meet domestic demands, but had a substantial surplus for export to Tibet. British-Indian revenue records show that copper mining was extensive and of high enough quality to compete on the Calcutta market. Brass work and papermaking were then more important than today. Nepal had provided both the artisans and the metal for manufacturing many of the images adorning the homes, monasteries, and temples of Tibet. The manufacture of small arms and cannon increased rapidly after the unification of Nepal under the Shah dynasty. In the mid-nineteenth century, it was estimated that these arsenals could equip forty-five battalions —a very substantial force in the Himalayas in those days.

Little of this preindustrial manufacturing base survived the nineteenth century. Homespun textiles could not compete with imports of manufactured cloth. Mining declined. The armaments industry virtually disappeared in the early years of the twentieth century when the British decided that the wiser and safer course was to accede to long-standing Nepali desires to be provided with British armaments.

This downward trend continued until 1932, when Juddha Shamsher succeeded to the prime ministership and inaugurated a new policy. Some encouragement was given to the previously banned Gandhian type of cottage industry program. In 1934, the Banijya Bardhak Samstha (Organization for the Development of Commerce), later renamed the Udyog Parishad (Industry Board), was founded. Two years later, the first bank—the Nepal Bank, Ltd.—was established, in part as a source of credit for industrial enterprises. That same year a Company Law was enacted which for the first time permitted joint stock enterprises. Within a few years, a successful jute mill was operating in Biratnagar and a match factory in Birgunj. The shortages caused by World War II provided further stimulus to Nepal's industrial development. Several cotton and jute mills, and sugar, paper, ceramics, glass, and chemical factories were established, most of them in the Terai. Nepali capital played a minor role, however, as most of these enterprises were Indian owned and managed. The Ranas, prudently hedging against a sudden adverse turn in their political fortunes, preferred to invest their capital surpluses outside of Nepal. Most other Nepalis continued to prefer investment in land. Thus no Nepali entrepreneurial or managerial class emerged to keep pace with the spurt in industrial development.

With the end of World War II, the prospects for further industrial progress seemed good. Between 1945 and 1949, several new joint stock enterprises were projected, and existing companies planned to expand their capacity. None of these ventures reached fruition, however, and indeed several factories were forced to close or reduce production. The abnormal conditions under which these industries had been established had permitted the existence of an inefficient managerial system, and abuses of the joint stock system were widespread. Credit facilities in Nepal were still sadly lacking, as the Nepal Bank, Ltd. had neither the resources nor the inclination to serve this purpose. Also, by 1949, competition from Indian and foreign industries had increased, and Nepali industries found themselves in a decidedly inferior position.

To cope with these developments, a new Company Law was promulgated in 1950, providing the government with extensive powers over the "managing agent" system and over the floating of joint stock enterprises, which had been haphazard at best. Strict application of some provisions of this law was, however, a difficult matter, and would have forced several existing industries to close—obviously not a very sound solution to Nepal's industrialization problems.

In Nepal, as in most developing areas, industrialization is viewed as the panacea for all economic ills. Nepalis dream of transforming their mountain kingdom into the "Switzerland of Asia." But there has been little progress toward this goal, and prospects for substantial improvement are not particularly bright. The first Five Year Plan (1956–1961) emphasized assistance to cottage industries and existing industrial concerns rather than to new industries, though a joint Nepal-America Cooperative Service was established to encourage small-scale industry. In 1957, this institution was converted into the Industrial Development Center, and was given the additional assignment of providing technical assistance to medium-scale industries.

With the election of the Nepali Congress government in 1959, renewed emphasis was given to industrialization. The first detailed statement on industrial policy stressed the government's intention to assist directly in the establishment of new industries. The Nepal Industrial Development Corporation (N.I.D.C.), with an authorized capital of ten million rupees, was then formed to provide long-term loans to industries. The N.I.D.C. also assumed the duties of the Industrial Development Center in providing technical assistance to existing and projected industries.

The royal regime has continued the industrialization program, essentially along the lines projected by the Nepali Congress. The 1950 Company Act was amended substantially in 1961, and wholly revised in 1963, easing the regulations on industries. In 1962 an Industrial Enterprises Act was promulgated to improve the conditions under which both foreign and domestic capital can invest in Nepal. New industries are granted a ten-year exemption from income tax, and are permitted to spend up to 70 per cent of hard currency earnings for the import of machinery and spare parts. Foreign investors are annually allowed to repatriate as profits ten per cent of the capital in hard currency. In addition, a government controlled organization, the Sajha, was established to extend financial and other assistance to cooperative industrial and commercial undertakings.

The gulf between policy and implementation remains wide, however. Industrial and mining enterprises have not increased significantly, nor is a rapid expansion likely in the foreseeable future. A number of middle-sized industries have been set up since 1961, usually with the assistance of foreign aid programs: cigarette and sugar factories by the Russians; paper, brick, and leather factories by the Chinese; and several industrial estates encompassing small-scale private enterprises by the United States and India. Nepal is still heavily dependent upon foreign economic assistance for the modest industrialization program projected under the third plan (1965–1970). Most of this has had to come from external private investment as government foreign aid agencies have not shown a sustained interest in supporting industrial enterprises in Nepal.

In line with its general economic policy, the Nepal government has made a determined effort to diversify its industrialization program by seeking to attract foreign investment from other than Indian sources. The results so far have not been encouraging, however. Several Indian industrial and business interests are prepared to invest in Nepal if this can be accomplished on advantageous terms, including the assurance of ready access to the Indian market for the commodities produced. The Nepali authorities find themselves in a dilemma on this question. They want rapid industrialization, and realize the importance of Indian capital and management for this purpose; but at the same time they are reluctant to agree to anything that would further increase Nepal's economic dependence upon India. The bargaining on this issue has been hard and as yet inconclusive, with the result that Indian investment in Nepal's industrialization has never approached its potential.[5] While the Nepal government continues to place great verbal emphasis upon industrialization, it has had to recognize that economic progress and development will be determined far more by the success achieved in revitalizing and reorganizing agriculture.

Trade and Commerce

The affluence of Kathmandu Valley has traditionally been associated with trade and with the status of the valley cities as entrepôts in the trans-Himalayan trade system. After the Gorkha conquest of the valley, new taxes were imposed on this trade, along with a strict ban on the admission of foreign traders. This interference with established trade patterns was resented by Tibetan and British

[5] There have been some encouraging developments recently which may increase the pace of industrialization. There has been an unplanned but rapid expansion since 1961 of small-scale industries—mostly foodgrain and oil mills—in the Terai. Preliminary surveys by the Nepal government indicated that many of these enterprises are the result of investment by Indian entrepreneurs from across the border who are interested in taking advantage of Nepal's less restrictive regulations on foodgrain preparation and marketing. There has also been Indian investment in a number of small stainless steel and synthetic textile factories set up in Nepal since 1965. These enterprises import the required materials from abroad and then process them for resale across the border in India where there is a ready market. The Indian government has objected to this practice on the grounds that it is a way of circumventing New Delhi's highly restrictive import controls. See the article on this subject by the Indian Ambassador to Nepal, Raj Bahadur (*Rising Nepal,* June 15, 1969).

Indian traders alike, and attempts were made to circumvent Kathmandu. For a time it seemed that direct British-Tibetan trade links might be established, but for a variety of reasons these attempts failed. After the Nepal-China war of 1792, in any event, Tibetan borders were closed to the Indian trade agents of the East India Company. Kathmandu's position in Indo-Tibetan trade was restored and remained unchallenged for more than a century. The opening of an easier route to Tibet through Sikkim and the Chumbi Valley (in the wake of the Younghusband expedition, 1903–1905), however, wrought radical changes. Kalimpong rapidly replaced Kathmandu as the most important Indo-Tibetan trade entrepôt. Nepali mercantile houses in Tibet continued to prosper owing to their privileged position under the terms of the Nepal-Tibet Treaty of 1856, but most of their commerce was conducted via the Sikkim route, rather than through Kathmandu.

In these circumstances, Nepal's trade and commerce was directed increasingly toward India, which absorbed most of the country's exports and was the primary source for imports. The 1923 Treaty of Sagauli between Nepal and the British liberalized trading arrangements substantially, but also served to enhance Nepal's position as a commercial adjunct of British India. Although there had been some expectation in Nepal of gaining more favorable terms from independent India, the 1950 Trade Treaty retained the main features of the Sagauli Treaty. Resentment concerning indirect controls over Nepal's trading system, reserved by India in the 1950 Treaty, became a constant element in Nepali politics, but it was only in 1960 that the Nepali Congress government succeeded in negotiating more favorable terms with India.

The post-revolutionary governments in Nepal had also been seriously concerned with legitimizing the privileged position that Nepali traders had long enjoyed to the north of the Himalayas, but this had to await a political settlement with the new Chinese rulers of Tibet. In 1956, shortly after the resumption of diplomatic relations with Peking, a treaty regulating trade between Nepal and Tibet was signed, replacing the old treaty of 1856. There was no significant expansion in trade, however, as Kathmandu could not at that time compete with Gangtok and Kalimpong as an entrepôt for the substantial trade then flowing between India and Tibet.

The emergence of a major Sino-Indian border dispute after 1959 seemed to hold out the prospect of important trade advantages for Nepal because of the economic blockade India imposed on trade with Tibet via the other main channels of communication across the Himalayas. Kathmandu saw an opportunity to restore its former pre-eminence in the trans-Himalayan trade structure and, at the same time, gain a broader measure of economic independence from India. A Nepal-China agreement, concluded in October, 1961, provided for the construction of a road between Kathmandu and Tibet which Nepali officials predicted would provide the country with important new markets as well as alternative sources for manufactured goods and other imports. This seemed to be a reasonable conclusion, as Peking's willingness to finance and construct this expensive road had been due, at least in part, to the expectation that Nepal could be used to circumvent the Indian trade blockade. Nepal also signed new trade agreements with Peking in 1964, 1966, and 1968 and with

Pakistan in 1962 and 1963 which were intended to advance the trade diversification program.[6]

For a wide variety of reasons—political, economic and strategic—Kathmandu has not achieved even its minimal targets in this respect. Trade with Pakistan was never more than 10 per cent of the modest volume projected in the trade treaties and, following the 1965 Indo-Pakistani war, has declined even further. Direct trade with China proper (mostly channelled through India to take advantage of lower transportation costs) has expanded substantially in recent years, but this has been accompanied by an equally large decline in Nepal's entrepôt trade with Tibet. Kathmandu's expectations of serving as an intermediary in trans-Himalayan trade has proven to be an illusion, primarily because of India's opposition to the re-export of commodities that would strengthen and support the large Chinese military establishment in Tibet. As most of the goods the Chinese in Tibet are eager to obtain from Nepal must either be imported from India or through India, Kathmandu has had to agree to New Delhi's demand that a ban be imposed on the re-export of such commodities. As a result, the Kathmandu-Tibet road is now virtually unused, and trade between Nepal and Tibet is largely restricted to smuggling and the important but small-scale local trade between the inhabitants on both sides of the border.[7]

[6] National Planning Council, *Summary of His Majesty's Government Three Year Plan, 1962–1965* (Kathmandu, 1962), p. 5.

[7] One of the primary objectives of China in the more recent trade talks has been to eliminate private Nepali traders in Tibet and to replace them with direct state-to-state trade. By 1968, the Nepal gov-

In 1963, Nepal's trade with countries other than India was estimated to constitute no more than 3 per cent of its combined imports and exports. In 1970, this figure may have reached as high as 10 per cent,[8] but this trade has demonstrated little capacity to expand much further. The ultimate objective, according to one official Nepali source, was to redirect perhaps 25 per cent of Nepal's trade to countries other than India, but it was admitted that this was impractical under existing conditions.

The Nepal government has concluded, albeit reluctantly, that more economic advantages can be derived from improving the terms of trade with India than from its highly publicized but only moderately successful diversification program. Fortunately for Kathmandu, the Indian government has since 1963 demonstrated a better appreciation of Nepal's objections to the existing trade structure and has agreed to modify these to the extent India's interests will permit. The result has been a substantial expansion of Indo-Nepali trade—much greater indeed

---

ernment had closed down the trade agencies it had established in Tibet under the 1956 treaty with China, and the number of Nepali subjects resident in Tibet had fallen drastically (see Kuladharma Ratna, "Sino-Nepalese Trade," *Rising Nepal,* July 26, 1968). Peking has also moved to restrict the local trade carried on by the inhabitants of the Nepal-Tibet border area. In the 1968 trade talks, according to Foreign Minister Kirtinidhi Bisht, the Chinese refused to agree to the extension of the clause of the 1956 treaty under which this trade had been conducted (*Gorkhapatra,* August 13, 1968).

[8] Recent official trade figures show somewhere between 25 and 35 per cent of Nepal's trade with countries other than India. However, these statistics do not include the extensive "unofficial" trade between the Terai and India, which is estimated to bring the Indian proportion of Nepal's trade back up to the 85–90 per cent figure.

in absolute terms than Nepal's trade with the rest of the world—and a gradual but real improvement in the trade structure as far as Nepal is concerned. Diversification is still the objective, but Kathmandu's sense of urgency on this question would now appear to be much less than in the 1961–1962 period when relations with India on all levels were badly strained. Indeed, the negotiations leading up to the projected revision of the 1960 Trade Treaty in 1970 have been primarily concerned with improving the terms of trade between Nepal and India and only secondarily with trans-trade questions.

Planning and Economic Development

A few tentative gestures in the direction of planned economic development were made during the closing years of the Rana regime. In 1949, for example, a National Planning Board was established and instructed to prepare a 15-year plan. Surveys of agricultural and industrial conditions were undertaken in several districts. The results should have alarmed the Ranas, but nothing in the way of a plan ever emerged, and the Board disappeared after the 1950 revolution.

The men who led the movement against the Ranas were assertively "modern," and convinced of the virtues of economic planning. Nevertheless, no real efforts at planning were even attempted for nearly five years, probably because of the lack of the basic requirements for planning —a sophisticated administrative machinery and adequate statistics. The first Five-Year Plan was drafted and presented to the country in 1956, but this was more a political than an economic document. It contained statements of broad objectives, too vague and unrealistic to be meaningful, along with a compilation of economic development programs under the Indian and American aid programs. But it projected little in the way of new programs, and made no real attempt to control and direct the allocation of Nepal's meager capital and material resources.

The Nepali Congress government which came to power in mid-1959 virtually ignored the first Plan and prepared a new Two-Year Plan, to commence in 1961. The December, 1960, coup intervened, however, and the Plan was dropped. The royal regime was equally devoted to the principles of economic planning, and a newly appointed National Planning Council commenced deliberations on another draft. In 1962, a Three-Year Plan was presented to the country as an interim measure until a more comprehensive Five-Year Plan could be prepared and inaugurated in 1965.

The economic development program in the second Five-Year Plan concentrated on the agrarian sector, but also included provisions for a few medium-scale industrial enterprises and cottage and small-scale industries. As heretofore, the development program is largely dependent upon foreign aid. In the 1966–1967 budget estimates, for instance, nearly 60 per cent of the development expenditures were to be met from foreign aid sources. These totalled 216 million rupees (approximately 29 million dollars) divided among the major foreign aid programs as follows: 113 million from India, 48 million from the United States, 30 million from China, 18.5 million from the Soviet Union, and 6.5 million from other sources including the United Nations. Substantially larger sums were available from foreign aid sources, but this was estimated to be the maximum that could realistically be expended during the year in view of Nepal's still inadequate administrative machinery.

Nepal's contribution to the 1966–1967 development budget was set at 150 million rupees, on paper a substantial increase over previous years. In actual fact this figure is misleading, since only a small proportion of the Nepali allocation was expended during the fiscal year. In performance terms, therefore, approximately 85 per cent of the development budget continued to be dependent upon foreign aid, which was essentially the same proportion as in 1960–1961. While the size of the development budget has expanded rapidly, Nepal's sense of self-reliance has, if anything, declined in recent years, and the tendency to look automatically to foreign aid for the support of new development programs is still deeply ingrained.

This dependency upon foreign aid is evident in all aspects of Nepal's development program, but probably most obviously in those areas in which considerable progress has been achieved since 1951—i.e., the development of communication and power facilities. Every major road and power plant in Nepal is the product of foreign capital and technical assistance, with the Nepal government usually playing only a minor supporting role. Indeed, some cynics, both Nepali and foreign, attribute the comparative success of these projects to this fact. If their assessment is correct, then both the Nepal government and the foreign governments and agencies extending aid should be equally concerned. Certainly one of the essential criteria of economic development involves the capacity of the local authorities to plan and administer development projects, even those dependent upon external financial support. Nepal's political leaders, however, seem more inclined to point with pride to their success in persuading foreigners to assume these onerous tasks than in undertaking the hard work themselves.

The critical role foreign economic assistance plays in the development program has also vastly complicated the problem of planning. Nepal can never be certain that aid promised will actually be forthcoming, or that projects once initiated will continue to be supported. The cement factory first promised by the Chinese in 1956 and again in 1960, for instance, was cancelled in 1964 for "technical reasons." Dependence upon foreign assistance, in limiting freedom of action, not only wounds sensitive Nepali nationalism but also gives rise to fears that adroit manipulation of economic pressures might force modifications in the nonalignment policy upon which Nepal has staked its independence. To minimize this danger, Kathmandu has deliberately sought to balance the various donors against each other and encourage competition between them whenever possible.

While this policy has substantially increased the amount of foreign aid available to Nepal, it has also raised a problem no less consequential from the planning viewpoint: how to coordinate economic aid programs stemming from such divergent sources as the United States, India, the Soviet Union, and China, all of which may be presumed to have their own ideas and objectives in granting aid. Although the Nepal government is the only agency able to fit these aid projects into a coherent program, in practice the difficulties have proved formidable. Kathmandu cannot make demands, but can merely express preferences and compose lists of priorities. The 1965–1970 Five-Year Plan improved this situation somewhat by providing a basis upon which the government could attempt to bring order out of a multitude of disconnected aid projects. But here again, weaknesses in the administrative structure have obstructed progress, frustrating the best efforts of the planners. The projected decentralization of administration, it was hoped, would compensate for deficiencies and gaps in the bureaucratic machinery. In fact, however, it has further complicated the planning process and obstructed the implementation of programs because of the severe lack of trained personnel at the local and regional level.

Whenever any nation embarks upon the modernizing process, the balance between political and economic considerations is delicate—often critically so—and will vary not only from one country to another, but also within a given country from one time to another. The Ranas did little modernizing, but attempted to keep the country secluded. Nepal's present government, reversing these outworn tactics, is accepting assistance from all quarters, attempting to modernize while at the same time maintaining internal equilibrium through equalizing pressures from outside. It need not be discouraging and certainly should not be surprising if the balance between political and economic considerations often—and not only in Nepal—seems overweighted on the political side. In a situation as complex as that of Nepal, overemphasis of the technical might well represent a more serious imbalance.

6. Nepal's
International Relations

The origins and, indeed, the fundamental principles of current Nepali foreign policy can be traced back nearly two centuries to the period of the unification of the central Himalayan hill areas under the Gorkha dynasty. With this conquest it became necessary to forge, for the first time, what could be called a Nepali foreign policy, as contrasted with the separate and often conflicting policies of the various kingdoms and principalities which had previously been sheltered within this mountainous region. Prithvi Narayan Shah, the founder of modern Nepal, had learned from the circumstances of his own success that his new kingdom, despite its strategic location and the martial temperament of his followers, was by no means invulnerable. Prior to his death (in 1775), he included in his advice to his courtiers the following warning:

This Kingdom is like a tarul [yam] between two stones. Great friendship should be maintained with the Chinese Emperor. Friendship should also be maintained with the Emperor beyond the Southern Seas [i.e., the British], but he is very clever. He has kept India suppressed, and is entrenching himself on the plains. . . . One day that army will come. Do not engage in an offensive attack. Fighting should be conducted on a defensive basis.[1]

Contemporary Nepali nationalist opinion has found this advice sufficiently persuasive and meaningful to publicize it as "divine counsel," and to cite it in support of a policy based upon "equal friendship" with China and India. The advice was not heeded, however, by Prithvi Narayan's immediate successors, who became embroiled first in the north with the Tibetans and the Chinese, later in the west with the Sikhs, and eventually in the south with the British. By the time peace was signed with the British in 1816, Nepal's territorial boundaries, although reduced considerably from the high-water mark of Gorkha conquests, were extended far beyond the area held by Prithvi Narayan in 1770. Nevertheless, Nepali exploits had also brought upon the kingdom annoying obligations and restrictions imposed by both their Chinese and British neighbors. The essentials of Prithvi Narayan's foreign policy were therefore once again put into effect to the extent permitted by changed circumstances.

Prithvi Narayan, in the interests of the security of his own reign and the independence of his newly-won kingdom, had made his basic principle the fullest possible isolation of Nepal from alien influences, even at the cost of adverse economic consequences. He had made Nepal forbidden territory to British Indian commercial and diplomatic agents, and had levied prohibitive duties on trade both to and through his capital. Actually, British determi-

[1] Yogi Naraharinath and Baburam Acharya, eds., *Rashtrapita Shri 5 Bada Maharaja Prithvi Narayan Shah* (Father of the Nation, Five Times Illustrious Great Maharaja Prithvi Narayan Shah) (Kathmandu: Bageshwar Press, 1953), pp. 15–16.

nation to place their own agents in the Nepali capital was only increased by the advantages attained through Kathmandu's monopoly position in Indo-Tibetan trade. The 1814–1816 Anglo-Nepal war forced a weakening of Nepal's strict isolationist policy. Nevertheless, for approximately three decades the British Resident in Kathmandu and his small staff were kept in comparative isolation, and were subjected to intense surveillance and a vigorous campaign of deception.

These efforts at deception, although occasionally perceived as such, were successful in misleading the British for some years as to the nature of the relations between Nepal and China. Nepali statesmen deliberately exaggerated the degree of intimacy of this relationship, presumably on the assumption that the East India Company would prefer to avoid a major confrontation on the Himalayan frontier that might endanger more important British commercial interests in China proper. Meanwhile, the strength of the Nepali army was steadily increased. There were obvious limits to the efficacy of such a policy. The military build-up not only increased British suspicion of Nepal's intentions, but also, because of its political implications, aroused considerable internal opposition within Nepal. The most fatal flaw was that the policy depended not only upon deceiving the British as to Chinese involvement in Nepali affairs, but upon a China strong enough to make the implied threat of intervention effective. No sooner had Prime Minister Bhim Sen Thapa's enemies been able to effect his downfall (1837), than it began to become obvious that China was in no position to intervene in Nepal even had it cared to do so. For nearly a decade after the fall of Bhim Sen Thapa, Nepal experienced a series of weak and unstable governments whose foreign policies displayed a shifting opportunism tinctured with an occasional adventurism which brought the country into disrepute with all its neighbors.

With the re-emergence of strong rule under Jang Bahadur, founder of the Rana regime, Nepali foreign policy was soon reformulated in the light of the knowledge he had obtained during his visit to Great Britain and to France in 1850–1851. China no longer constituted an effective counterbalance to British India. Although relations with Peking continued, only two of the periodic missions were sent out from Kathmandu during the thirty-one-year rule of Jang Bahadur, and of these only the first was allowed to proceed to Peking. Under Jang Bahadur the Nepali army was kept strong, but great care was taken to avoid arousing apprehension in India as to Nepal's role in inter-Himalayan and Indian politics. Indeed, Jang Bahadur led troops into battle on the British side during the 1857 uprising in India.

The British had long been impressed by the fighting qualities of the Nepali hill men, but preferred to utilize their services as recruits in Indian Army regiments, trained and commanded by British officers, rather than as an allied army under independent command. It soon became a primary objective of British policy toward Nepal to obtain the right to recuit "Gurkha" soldiers openly within Nepal. Jang Bahadur was able to resist British pressure, but succession quarrels after his death gave the British leverage which they did not hesitate to use. Bir Shamsher, faced with the alternative of British support for the rival faction, the sons of Jang Bahadur, reluctantly gave in. But the British, once their objective was gained, proved generous. Over the years an accommodation was reached which brought the basic interests of the Ranas and the British into remarkable harmony. British India paid a subsidy to the government of Nepal for soldiers recruited, and in due course pension money brought a flow of cash into the most remote Nepali villages. The British guided Nepali foreign policy, but the Rana regime enjoyed complete internal autonomy, while assured of British support against both internal subversion and external aggression. The Ranas received complete cooperation from the British in the retention and implementation of the isolationist policy which banned foreigners from all areas of the country except Kathmandu, and which limited Nepal's international relations to those with British India, Tibet, and, until 1912, China.

The Ranas have been bitterly criticized by contemporary nationalist opinion in Nepal for accepting an inferior status with respect to British India which, it is charged, hampered Nepal's economic and political modernization. This criticism appears somewhat wide of the mark. As nationalists, they are presumably not making the argument that Nepal would today be more advanced had it been a British colony rather than a small (though valued) British ally, although there is much that might be said in favor of such an argument. On the other hand, it was no necessary corollary of Rana foreign policy that the Ranas should have made their identification with British ruling classes so complete that they became alienated from their own subjects. It was not Rana foreign policy which made their regime vulnerable to British withdrawal from India, but Rana internal policy—the utter tenacity with which they refused to share their political, economic, and cultural privileges.

The isolationist policy—accepted and even encouraged by the British, whose interests it also served—remained in effect until British withdrawal from India became imminent in 1947. Nepal then began a number of moves to achieve international recognition. Goodwill missions from the United States and Nationalist China were received in 1946, and return missions sent to both Washington and Nanking that same year. Nepal's legation in London was raised to embassy status; [2] a Nepali delegation attended the Asian Conference in New Delhi in March, 1947, marking Nepal's first participation in an international conference; in April, diplomatic relations were established by treaty with the United States.

Efforts to achieve international recognition continued at an accelerated pace during succeeding years. Admission to the United Nations was debarred by Soviet veto until December, 1955, but recognition had been accorded by many nations on an individual basis long before the U.N. was free to act. Today Nepal maintains diplomatic relations with virtually all major nations, and plays an independent role in regional associations. The old policy of maintaining independence by universal exclusion has been replaced by a policy of admitting all comers on approximately equal terms.[3] Yet now, no less than in the days of Prithvi Narayan, the major foreign policy problem faced by Nepali administrators is the maintenance of the desired balance in relations with both India and China.

[2] The legation had been established in 1934. The timing suggests that the rulers of both Nepal and Great Britain thought it prudent to establish direct relations between Kathmandu and London, in the context of the broad degree of self-government which the nationalist movement in India then appeared to be on the verge of obtaining.

[3] Certain formalities are waived with respect to Indian nationals.

Such a balance would not have presented too many problems had, for example, mainland China remained under the domination of the Kuomintang government; or had the Chinese Communists placed the same value as did Nehru on Sino-Indian friendship; or even, given mutual hostility between these neighboring giants, had the military power which each could bring to bear on their Himalayan frontier been of comparable magnitude. But developments were not to fall into such clear-cut patterns.

In 1946, the Rana government had responded favorably to the Chinese Nationalist overtures for the re-establishment of diplomatic relations. Before this could be accomplished, however, Chiang Kai-shek's government had collapsed and the Chinese Communists had emerged as the new ruling power in China. With British power removed from India and the Chinese Communist regime an uncertain factor in Himalayan area politics, the Ranas decided to fall back on their previous policy of establishing Nepal as a valuable Indian ally. During the Hyderabad and Kashmir incidents, for example, ten battalions of the Nepal State Army were dispatched to India's assistance at the latter's request.

The Communist victory in China, accompanied as it was by threats against Tibet and proclamations of intent to re-establish China's "traditional boundaries," [4] brought Nepal and India close together. Treaties were quickly signed (1950) which replaced Nepal's old treaties with

[4] "Traditional boundaries" were left officially undefined, but in the more exuberant unofficial nationalist outpourings these were not only equated with the high-water mark of real or imagined imperial conquest, but were also taken to include Bhutan, Sikkim, and Nepal, as well as Tibet.

Great Britain, with secret clauses attached which bound the two governments to mutual consultation in case either was threatened by an outside power.

The basic features of Nepal's foreign policy did not change significantly after the revolution of 1951, although the terminology used to describe the policy did. Nehru was at this time formulating in more precise terms the principles of "nonalignment" and "peaceful coexistence," and Nepal adopted the fundamentals of Indian foreign policy as its own. Initially this may have been a reflection of Indian influence, but it is also evident that these terms came to describe Nepal's foreign policy objectives very well. Note that Kathmandu has adhered to these principles more stubbornly than ever in recent years, even after Indian influence in Nepal suffered a sharp decline.

King Mahendra's ascension to the throne in 1955 marked another significant milestone in Nepal's international relations. The new monarch's approach to international politics was as strikingly different from that of his predecessor as it was on domestic policy. King Tribhuvan had close personal and family ties with India and with several Indian leaders. Nepal's most intimate cultural, religious, and ideological bonds were with its southern neighbor. In strengthening these ties, King Tribhuvan saw no threat to Nepal's independence, but rather a promise of favorable conditions for Nepal's rapid progress. During his reign, both Kathmandu and New Delhi accepted the "special relationship" between the two countries as an inescapable fact, and indeed as an advantage to both.

King Mahendra's approach to Indo-Nepali relations was quite different since he shared the sentiments of the younger educated Nepalis (concentrated in Kathmandu) whose views of national sovereignty often tended to be un-compromising in conception and anti-Indian in action. From this perspective, Indian influence in all spheres of Nepali life is considered so overwhelming as to constitute a debasement of Nepal's national identity. If sovereignty were to have any substance, the argument ran, the all-embracing pervasiveness of Indian influence in the political, social and economic life of the country had to be sharply reduced so that it no longer was decisive in determining the course of developments. It should be understood that even the most vehement Nepali nationalists did not imagine that their country could or should be isolated entirely from India; nor did many of them contemplate throwing Nepal into the arms of a third power to spite India, although they occasionally talked in such terms. Their objective was fuller independence, and under existing conditions this could only be achieved by diminishing the intimacy of the relationship with India and concurrently expanding ties with the rest of the world. This frame of reference must be kept clearly in view if the sometimes bewildering twists and turns in Nepali foreign policy in the post-1955 period are to be comprehended.

The first year of King Mahendra's reign was largely devoted to internal politics and it was only in 1956 that a new trend in foreign policy became evident. The first indication of impending change was the appointment of Tanka Prasad Acharya as Prime Minister in January, 1956. Tanka Prasad had a reputation as a "leftist" and as a strong supporter of closer relations with Communist China. This reputation was enhanced almost immediately on his appointment, when in his first press conference, he specifically rejected the concept of a "special relationship" with India and substituted in its place the slogan of "equal friendship with all." The Communist Party of Nepal was legalized, an agreement was signed with China on Tibet, and Chinese and Russian economic assistance was sought and obtained—or at least promised.

These policies were all introduced under the aegis of the Tanka Prasad government, but it would probably be a mistake to attribute them to the Prime Minister. The initial overtures that finally led to the Sino-Nepali treaty and economic aid agreement had been made before Tanka Prasad assumed office. Indeed, the Chinese Communist conquest of Tibet had in effect abrogated the 1856 treaty which had formerly governed relations between Nepal and Tibet, and had made an eventual settlement with Peking inevitable. Once India had signed an agreement with China (April, 1954) recognizing the latter's status in Tibet, Nepal could not long delay. There is every reason for assuming that Tanka Prasad's China policy was not only King Mahendra's policy, but had also been actively encouraged by India initially. New Delhi's approbation, however, changed to intense concern when it discovered that Peking was no longer content to accept Nepal as an exclusive Indian sphere of influence, but was determined to compete with India for influence throughout the entire Himalayan region.

The victory of the Nepali Congress in the 1959 general elections marked the commencement of yet another phase in Nepali foreign policy. The Nepali Congress cabinet assumed office in June, 1959, coinciding with the outbreak of a widespread anti-Chinese revolt in central Tibet and the emergence of a major Sino-Indian border dispute over Ladakh. Kathmandu was forced into several fundamental policy decisions which might otherwise have been avoided or at least postponed. The previous assumption that Sino-Indian relations would be conducted within limits set by mutual regard for "peaceful coexistence" had been opened to serious question.

In these circumstances, the Nepali Congress cabinet attempted to adhere to the basic foreign policy principles that had been applied since 1955, but with some subtle, usually unstated reinterpretations. It was the government's firm intention to maintain friendly relations with China, and indeed to seek an accommodation with Peking on all issues outstanding between the two countries. B. P. Koirala, for example, initiated the negotiations with Peking over the Nepal-Tibet boundary that culminated in the 1961 Sino-Nepal border treaty. If possible, Nepal hoped to avoid disputes over boundaries similar to those that were currently impairing Sino-Indian relations. The government may well have expected, also, that more favorable terms could be arranged with China while that country was engaged in a major dispute with India than under less critical conditions.

If the Nepali Congress government was careful to maintain friendly relations with China, it was no less careful to avoid action that might substantially increase Chinese Communist influence in Nepal. Chou En-Lai's proposal of a road connecting Kathmandu with Tibet was rejected.[5] It may also have been more than coincidental that none of the Chinese-aided economic development projects provided in the 1956 agreement ever got under way during this period.

It is apparent that B. P. Koirala and his colleagues did

[5] *Asian Recorder,* December 3–9, 1961, p. 4298.

not accept Chinese professions of goodwill and friendship at their face value. Unlike previous Nepali governments, which had tended to dismiss—at least publicly—any suggestions that China might be a potential threat to Nepal, the Nepali Congress attempted to underline, if somewhat obliquely, the seriousness of the potential threat. The party's statement on the revolt in Tibet, for instance, which was issued in April, 1959, by the two General-Secretaries of the party, strongly denounced Chinese policy in Tibet. In marked contrast to official Nepali policy, this statement contained the implication that the Chinese were not in Tibet as lawful sovereigns but only as a consequence of their recent conquest. Since the two party secretaries had also been assigned ministerial posts in the government then being formed, questions arose as to a shift in official policy. B. P. Koirala was obliged to explain that this statement represented the viewpoint of the party rather than of his government. Nevertheless, the statement certainly reflected the attitude of many members of the government, and constituted the first instance in which a high, semi-official source in Nepal had implicitly characterized the Peking regime as aggressive.

Perhaps even more indicative of the B. P. Koirala government's attitude toward China was the position assumed on the two incidents that threatened to disrupt relations between the two countries in 1960. The first of these concerned China's sudden and unexpected claim to Mt. Everest, while the other centered around a border firing in which a Nepali frontier guard was killed by Chinese troops in territory which Peking later conceded belonged to Nepal. In both instances, China attempted to minimize the seriousness of these incidents, and to mollify Nepali public opinion by evasive statements which seemed to concede the Nepali position but which did not actually abandon the Chinese case. The Nepali Congress government refused to be satisfied with meaningless gestures and instead attempted to stress the long-range implications of these developments. Here again, the Congress leaders seemed to be emphasizing the potential Chinese threat to Nepal.

What the B. P. Koirala government was attempting, presumably, was to encourage a more balanced approach in the public's attitudes toward China and India, and to counter the tendency among some Nepali nationalists to assume that India constituted the *only* threat to Nepal's independence. The situation on the border was evidently serious enough to convince most Nepali Congress leaders that anti-Indian agitation, which they themselves had earlier not been adverse to encouraging, had become extremely dangerous, serving only the purposes of China and the Nepali Communists. While there was no intention of abandoning the "nonalignment" policy, which in Nepal is interpreted to mean primarily nonalignment in the Sino-Indian dispute, the implication of some Nepali Congress statements and actions indicated that, if a choice had to be made, Nepal could only align itself with India.

This implicitly pro-Indian orientation was also evident in the quietly efficient way in which the Congress cabinet sought to settle some of the outstanding issues between India and Nepal that had long antagonized Nepali opinion. The 1960 amendment of the 1950 Trade Treaty, and the agreement on the Gandaki river project, were steps in this direction. What was particularly novel in this and similar situations was the absence of anti-Indian propa-

ganda as one form of pressure upon New Delhi to accede
to Nepali proposals.

This phase of Nepali foreign policy was abruptly reversed following the sudden dismissal of the Nepali Congress government in December, 1960. What part foreign
policy considerations may have played in instigating the
coup has not yet been clarified. Afterwards, King Mahendra made oblique references to "antinational" plots, but
his charges were not made specific. It cannot be said
whether these comments were primarily intended to gain
internal support through the exploitation of a popular nationalist issue, or whether they reflected a deep-seated suspicion that the Nepali Congress government had indeed
subverted some of the basic foreign policy principles
which the King had formulated in 1955. It is equally possible that he was applying lessons from his knowledge of
Nepali history, and was moving primarily to protect his
own position. In any event, he quickly reinstituted his earlier policy, and a shocked India responded sharply.

In retrospect, it appears likely that New Delhi and
Kathmandu each seriously miscalculated the intentions
and objectives of the other in the period following the December coup. The royal regime appeared to give undue
weight to the expression of Indian displeasure—heavily
played up in the press of both countries—and did not take
into sufficient account the consistency of India's policy toward the Himalayan states. Since 1947 this policy had
shown little influence of ideological considerations. New
Delhi had considered Indian security best bulwarked by
stability in the strategic frontier area, and had been ready
to support any regime that offered continuity combined
with sensitivity toward necessary reform. India had been

prepared to accept royal autocracy in Bhutan and Sikkim. Even the Rana regime had been acceptable until it had reached the verge of internal collapse. Indian dismay at the unseating of the Nepali Congress government was essentially a measure of New Delhi's anxiety over Nepal's past instability and of the Indian belief that the Nepali Congress had at long last provided a government that could bring stability and progress to Nepal. There was no reason to assume that India's basic policy toward the Himalayan area would change, but somehow this was not made clear in Kathmandu.

What seems to have happened next is that New Delhi and Kathmandu lost sight of the legitimate fears and anxieties of the other government, and the measures that each took to allay its own anxieties gave the appearance of confirming the worst suspicions of the other. Thus, almost simultaneously, in the fall of 1961, Nepali political refugees in India threatened to launch a direct action campaign against King Mahendra, and the King signed an agreement with China for a road which would for the first time breach the Himalayan barrier and connect Kathmandu with Tibet by means of motor transport.

New Delhi, which may at first have seriously underestimated the strength and resilience of the royal regime, was caught in a dilemma. Any overt support to the rebels might force King Mahendra even closer to the Chinese, while acceptance of the King's terms—strict supervision of Nepali Congress leaders and workers in India—might eventually force the opposition within Nepal to turn to China for support and guidance. The Indian government attempted to maintain ties with both the royal regime and the Nepali Congress, refusing either to place rebel leaders under close police supervision, or to give them diplomatic or material assistance in their attempts to overthrow the royal regime. Both Nepal and India brought economic pressures to bear, India attempting to reverse the trend of Nepal's foreign policy, and Nepal attempting to reduce economic dependence upon India through the development of alternative sources of trade and aid. This situation had just reached a critical stage when, in October, 1962, the Chinese launched attacks on Indian territory, forcing both Nepal and India to reappraise their policies.

A reconciliation took place with surprising smoothness, considering the undiplomatic language which had occasionally characterized the exchanges between New Delhi and Kathmandu earlier in 1962. It seems probable that Indo-Nepali relations had not really deteriorated to the extent suggested by these verbal outbursts, which were, at least in part, a façade behind which the two governments conducted a dialogue on more basic issues that neither side, for its own reasons, wished to bring into the open, but which both understood. Neither government was interested in pushing their disagreements beyond a certain point. When India moved to improve relations with Nepal at the time of the Sino-Indian border war, in October, 1962, there was a total cessation of notes and statements of the type that had been exchanged at a furious rate only a few days earlier.

Subsequent developments tended to ease tensions. In December, 1962, on the advice of the Indian government, Nepali Congress leaders residing in India terminated their "direct action" movement. King Mahendra thus obtained the tacit guarantee from New Delhi that he considered essential to the stability of his regime. Both governments appeared to become more aware of their mutual interdependence and more willing to acknowledge each other's vital needs. Although issues remained on which national interests as defined by Nepal were at variance with goals pursued by India, for some years both sides, as if by mutual consent, avoided direct confrontation on issues where agreement was lacking.

It was not to be expected, however, that those policies considered by Kathmandu to be essential either to economic development or to political independence would be reversed, short of an extreme emergency. The effort to minimize differences and accentuate similarities in outlook has not met with total success. In mid-1969, for example, chronic Nepali irritation over some aspects of the *de facto* association with India on defense and security matters reached crisis proportions as a result of relatively minor disagreements involving a small-scale border dispute and an official Indian ban on the import of certain Nepali products. Obviously, neither side can take for granted the accommodation between the two countries so painfully achieved during the past decade, nor presume that further basic modifications in their terms of relationship are unnecessary.

Despite internal satisfaction with the remodeling of Nepal's foreign policy along lines more compatible with national pride, it is still uncertain whether the strains inherent in the country's difficult geopolitical situation have been significantly eased. There can be no doubt, however, that Kathmandu has developed an impressive repertory of responses to the unwelcome intrusion of external influences, whether these stem from India, China, the West, or the Soviet Union. The tactics utilized are classic in type: an intricate and careful balancing of external forces combined with a cautious tacking back and forth between the two most proximate of these powers, India and China. The objective has been to minimize the restrictions imposed on Nepal's freedom of action while at the same time maximizing the state's internal and external security.

Balance has been sought in two ways: through nonalignment in the Sino-Indian rivalry for leadership in the Himalayan area, and through a process of political and economic diversification that would alleviate Nepal's semi-satellite relationship to India. Nonalignment, when first adopted as a basic principle of Nepali foreign policy in 1951, was more an expression of confidence in Indian leadership in international affairs than a more narrowly conceived response to Nepal's self interest. The Chinese Communist take-over in Tibet soon opened for Nepal the possibility of resuming a buffer-state role not too dissimilar from that played in the previous century. Gradually, however, Kathmandu came to conceive its role more as a link between ideologically disparate but basically friendly neighbors. This implied a change in the terms of Nepal's relationships with both India and China.

With the outbreak of the Sino-Indian border dispute in 1959 the link concept lost its utility, but a newly defined buffer concept was introduced as the foundation of Nepali foreign policy. No longer was Nepal's buffer role merely a convenience for India, as it had tended to be earlier, but rather it became in part the product of a balance that Nepal itself had helped to create. With the slogan of "equal friendship for all," nonalignment became both a symbol of Nepal's national sovereignty and a means for guarding its integrity against external influences. This guise has not always been easy for Nepal to maintain, since in some respects the "special relationship" with India still exists and cannot readily be disowned. Nevertheless, the general trend of Nepali foreign policy under the royal regime has been toward a more literal definition of nonalignment, and this trend can be expected to continue as long as the situation in the Himalayan area remains sufficiently fluid.

In pursuing this neutral course in the face of Sino-Indian confrontation, Nepal has had to accept certain limitations on its own freedom of action. Where difficult choices have arisen, national priorities have emerged more clearly. The royal regime has more than once demonstrated, for example, that under present conditions the search for fuller sovereignty has priority over purely defensive contingencies. King Mahendra has seen the answer to Nepal's security and identity problems in nonalignment and "Nepalization"—the adoption of a political system differing from both China's Communist regime and India's parliamentary democracy.

King Mahendra's impressive achievements in the sphere of foreign policy have strengthened the position of the regime internally and have enhanced its international prestige, but Nepal still remains a small, relatively weak country, wedged between two vastly more powerful states whose bitter contest for power and influence extends far beyond the Himalayan region. The freedom of choice allowed to Nepal is therefore strictly limited by the exigencies of power politics. Concessions have been extracted from both sides through the adroit manipulation of Nepal's strategic location, but in the long run they are likely to

mean very little except in the context of a compromise settlement involving all the participant powers. In the absence of such a settlement, Nepal's independence is best
served by an approximate balance of power and influence
between its great neighbors. Nepal lacks the capacity to
ensure the maintenance of that balance, but conceivably
could, through serious errors in judgment, endanger both
its own independence and the peace of the long Sino-Indian frontier.

7. Modernizing
Nepali Politics

The transitional stage in the process of political modernization in Nepal commenced with the overthrow of the Rana regime in 1951. Earlier political developments had often involved changes in leadership within the existing political structure, but had only rarely affected the political process itself—that is, the method by which political positions were gained and decisions made. "Traditional" politics in Nepal had emerged from a long-term, although not necessarily peaceful, counterpoising of the interests of four elements in Nepali society: the royal family and its various collateral branches; those sections of the Brahman caste that performed certain religious, judicial, and astrological functions for the state and ruling families; the military and landholding aristocracy, mostly of Kshatriya caste status, at both the local and central level; and the Newar commercial caste families who dominated the trading system and the middle levels of the bureaucracy. The balance among these groups, or more frequently factions within these groups, varied from time to time. But until 1951, politics was their preserve and, as noted earlier, was conducted almost exclusively along familial lines.

The 1950–1951 revolution, "unfinished" though it may have been, marked a new departure in Nepali politics. It

Hallward Library - Issue Receipt

Customer name: Sitkowska, Florentyna

Title: Politics in Nepal : a study of post-Rana
political developments and party politics / by
Anirudha Gup
ID: 1000778580
Due: 02/04/2015 23:59

Title: The cultural politics of markets : economic
liberalization and social change in Nepal /
Katharine Ne
ID: 1006570755
Due: 02/04/2015 23:59

Total items: 2
05/02/2015 13:54

All items must be returned before the due date
and time.
The Loan period may be shortened if the item is
requested.

WWW.nottingham.ac.uk/is

was truly revolutionary, at least in the limited sense that it constituted an extrasystemic change which radically transformed the political process and the pattern of political behavior. It also brought a whole new cast of characters to the political stage, for the revolution was carried out under the leadership of a "modernizing" elite, some of whose origins and forms of group identification lay outside the traditional ruling elite. Even the revolutionary leaders who did nominally belong to the classes which had traditionally dominated the social, political, and economic structure in Nepal came from families that were outside the mainstream. Many others of their associates were from groups which had hitherto been kept on the periphery of the Nepali political process—Magars, Gurungs, Limbus, Kiratis, and Nepali citizens of Indian descent from the Terai. Perhaps the most striking aspect of this new political elite was the relative absence of members of the Kshatriya caste, from whose ranks the agents of change had usually been drawn in the past. This may help explain why individuals from this group have played the most prominent role in the politics of Nepal since the royal coup of December, 1960.

The importance of the modernizing elite in the period after the 1950 revolution was greatly enhanced by the sudden and wholesale intrusion of external influences, primarily from India, which left the traditional political process in a state of disarray. The rigorously enforced isolation policy of the Rana regime had been remarkably successful, on the whole, in insulating Nepal from the trauma of nationalist politics that had disrupted India periodically since the first world war. Many members of the new modernizing elite had served an apprenticeship in India and were deeply imbued with the spirit and ideology of Indian nationalist politics. The political system they sought to introduce was neither an evolution from, nor a modification of, the traditional Nepali political process, but an alien system whose basic linkages were with the politics of post-independent India. The 1951 Interim Government of Nepal Act, for instance, which most closely reflected the political ideology of this group, was an indifferently disguised adaptation of the 1950 Indian Constitution. As such, it completely ignored both the very different political and social backgrounds of the two countries and their dissimilar historical and cultural backgrounds. What was natural and proper for the political public of India, experienced as they were in the politics of party organization, was often radically innovative and alien in Nepal. Since most of the Nepali political elite in 1951 had not had the advantage of long exposure to the political mores and tactics of the Indian nationalist movement, they felt distinctly uncomfortable and ill at ease in this strange political milieu even in those cases in which they were not opposed to its ultimate objectives.

The innovative efforts of the modernizing elite appeared to meet with a substantial degree of success in the immediate post-revolutionary period. For a time, the traditional process and pattern of political behavior was overshadowed by a system of politics based, at least ostensibly, upon party organizations that made some pretense of operating on a mass scale. The traditional familial basis of political association receded in importance, although it never disappeared. Nonfamilial forms of political factionalism emerged, founded in a few instances on ideological considerations but far more frequently on economic and social interests affecting caste, community, or region.

This new brand of politics had to overcome strong resistance from a wide variety of sources. Numerous factors inherent in Nepal's history and in the dynamics of its social and administrative systems blunted the impact of these innovations and gradually reshaped them into patterns that conformed better to traditional Nepali values and methods of operation. Neither the political nor the economic infrastructure of a democratic system of politics existed in Nepal in 1951, and indeed the very concept and values of a democratic polity were as alien to the general populace as it was to most of the traditional elite. The popular view of government was intrinsically authoritarian, in the orthodox Hindu interpretation of that term under which politics was perceived to be the preserve of men of inherently superior status who ruled by right of their high-caste origin. There may have been widespread discontent with certain aspects of this system, but opposition to its basic principles was seldom articulated on the popular level, or even by the modernizing elite in conceptual terminology that made much sense to the *duniyadar* (common man). The new democratic image of government as an instrument subjected to popular control by means of a universally participatory political process was slow to gain acceptance outside of that small group of Nepalis who had been educated in western-style institutions in India and Nepal. In the critical transitional period from 1951 to 1959, there was no substantial popular support from either the traditional elite or the broader public for the few ill-conceived efforts to introduce and sustain democratic institutions and processes.

Unfortunately for the success of the experiment, even among the modernizing elite, concepts of political responsibility did not develop as rapidly as involvement in politics and a preoccupation with self-aggrandizement. Indeed, one of the most serious deficiencies of the democratic movement in post-1951 Nepal was the failure of the agents of political change to reach a consensus, no matter how ambiguous, upon the forms and values of the innovations they were theoretically committed to introduce. The absence of a well-articulated ideology of political modernization was perhaps most apparent during the period in office (1951–1952) of the first Nepali Congress government headed by M. P. Koirala. The party of the revolution found itself supporting, if somewhat unwillingly, a ministry headed by a prime minister instinctively unsympathetic to many of the proclaimed goals of the revolution and who considered his own role as that of a protector of public order until the long process of constitution-making had been completed. The bifurcation of the revolutionary movement, as represented by the split in the Nepali Congress in 1952, has generally been interpreted as the consequence of personality clashes, particularly between the Koirala half brothers, but it also reflected a serious division within the modernizing elite over its ultimate objectives. This ambivalence within the Nepali Congress had largely disappeared by the time the B. P. Koirala government took office in 1959, but developments elsewhere within the political system made this painfully-achieved consensus of less significance than it would have been a decade earlier.

The political party competitors of the Nepali Congress were, if anything, more confused about their political goals and more equivocal about their status as agents of change. While they were usually ardent proponents of democratization and constitutional monarchy on the public platform, their role in the political process was often that of a saboteur of developments in this direction that did not seem to serve their immediate interests. A self-proclaimed leftist and amateur Marxist such as Tanka Prasad Acharya, for instance, led the movement to transform the first general elections into a contest for the selection of a parliament, operating under a constitution granted by the king, rather than a constituent assembly empowered to create a new polity. Again, in December, 1960, he and virtually all other opposition party leaders applauded the dismissal of the Nepali Congress government and the abrogation of the parliamentary system, presumably because they had fared much worse under an elective system than under a palace-centered political process.

The failure of the political parties to achieve a consensus on a program of political democratization and to operate on that basis would have been less serious if that other potential institutional agent of change, the central bureaucracy, had played a more active role. In fact, however, the reorganization of the administrative system that followed the 1950–1951 revolution proved to be a negligible factor in the process of political modernization. A number of "modernists" were absorbed into the administration, but most of them quickly adapted themselves to the prevailing rules of the game. Traditionally, promotion —and even security of tenure—within the bureaucracy had been based upon ascriptive, primarily familial, considerations rather than upon achievement or devotion to duty. The pattern of ascription has changed in certain respects since 1951, as political rather than familial affiliations are now probably more important, but a merit system has never been introduced.

The influx into the administration in recent years of a large number of young educated Nepalis with distinctly modernist views has not, as yet, made much of an impact on the general character of the administrative system, since they have had to accept the established operating procedures if they were to have any chance for survival in that incredibly complex and competitive institution. We can presume that, behind the scenes, they are slowly reshaping the bureaucracy along lines that they find more compatible and that eventually major changes will be affected even in that most resistant of institutions. But until now, the bureaucracy has been at best a neutral factor in the process of political, social, and economic innovation, overresponsive to momentary shifts in political leadership and insufficiently aware of its potential as an agency of modernization. Rather we have had the curious spectacle of an institution dominated by men who are often modernist and innovative in outlook, but which nevertheless has generally served as a bulwark against change and for the preservation of the status quo.

The crucial point in the contest between what were essentially innovative and traditional forces in Nepali politics was reached with the accession of King Mahendra to the throne in 1955. The new monarch quickly demonstrated a tenacious capacity to exploit certain aspects of both the traditional and innovative political processes in furthering his own political goals. The parliamentary system established under the provisions of the 1959 Constitution, during which some of the innovative features of post-1951 politics appeared on the verge of reaching fruition, proved to be only a brief interlude. With the dismissal of the Nepali Congress government and the abrogation of the 1959 Constitution, the King renewed and intensified his efforts to evolve a political system that was suited to objective conditions in Nepal but at the same time preserved and expanded the role of the throne as the source of political authority and as the articulator of Nepal's political consensus.

King Mahendra's approach to politics could be described as counter-innovational in the sense that it conflicts with some of the fundamental aspects of the political changes introduced after 1951. The objective of a dynamic, authoritarian, politically-active monarchical system which shares power with other levels and institutions of government only on minor, nonessential (that is, nonessential to the palace) matters has been incorporated as the basic feature of the 1962 Constitution—in effect gaining for the King the position formerly held by the Rana prime minister. And indeed, there are other obvious similarities between post-1960 and pre-1951 politics in Nepal which distinguish both periods from the interim. Under the Ranas, political activity was confined almost exclusively within the narrow and stifling milieu of the court— i.e., the court of the Rana prime minister. While the courtier-politician did not disappear during the 1951–1960 period, his role was subsidiary to that of the new party leadership whose claims to authority and influence were based on the presumption of some degree of popular support. Since December, 1960, the party politician has vanished—except for illegal political action—and the courtier-politician once again dominates the scene with maneuvers and conspiracies centered around the royal palace.

The "traditional" and reactionary aspects of post-1960 politics in Nepal, however, should not disguise the fact that the King's political and economic programs have their own innovative features. The conceptual framework under which political change is now being accomplished may differ in some vital respects from the 1951 or 1959 periods, but change is nonetheless essential to the King's program. Mahendra's concept of the role of the monarchy, as it responds to the challenge of institutional adaptation and nation-building, bears little relationship to the functioning of that institution in any previous historical era since the protagonist of the Shah dynasty, Prithvi Narayan Shah, first established a unified state in the central Himalayas two centuries ago. Indeed, the monarchy has probably been a more effective modernizing force than the political parties, the bureaucracy, and perhaps even the educational institutions. While the 1962 constitutional infrastructure can scarcely be classified as democratic, neither is it authoritarian in the traditional manner, for it has broadened participation in the political process to some extent. New groups—such as non-Brahman, non-Kshatriya landowning elements—which had been largely confined to a local political role, have now been given an opportunity to participate in the political process at the national level via the panchayat system. Whether other less-favored outgroups in Nepali society will also be successfully politicized and a broadly participatory polity evolved, however, is still uncertain.

An inherent element in the process of modernization throughout much of the Afro-Asian world has been a tendency toward extreme political instability. In Nepal, as elsewhere, this is in part the result of the need to rationalize political and administrative systems and at the same time to engage in intensive nation-building activities.

While the two processes are probably closely interdependent in long-run terms, they do raise questions of priorities in societies engaged in this tiresome and often discouraging endeavor. There can be little doubt that for King Mahendra the nation-building program has first priority, since several of his more controversial policies seem to have been motivated by this consideration. One of the main factors behind the King's decision to abolish political parties in 1960, for instance, was his apprehension that the party system, which he described as corrupt, conflict-oriented, and faction-ridden, was disruptive of national unity.

King Mahendra has sought to circumvent this problem in his own political system by deliberately encouraging a task-oriented approach under which the emphasis is placed upon essentially technical considerations, the achievement of goals, while the crucial political function, the definition of goals, is retained as a royal prerogative. To accomplish this, he has had to emasculate all potential institutional rivals to the monarchy—the bureaucracy, the representative institutions, and all forms of voluntary political, economic, and social organizations—making them subservient to the palace even in the conduct of their normal functions. The basic premise, presumably, is that the complex tasks of political institutionalization can be safely ignored, or at least postponed, if certain minimal changes are effected in the country's economic and social systems. But this may prove to be a dangerous fallacy, particularly if the rate of economic change should prove to be more rapid than planned and accompanied by the mobilization of new social groups into the nation's political and economic matrix. The overall experience of countries more advanced on the road to modernization than Nepal has been that political institutionalization must occur concurrently, or preferably prior to qualitative changes in the economy and social structure, if some degree of political stability and continuity is to be achieved.[1]

In his perceptive essay on the role of traditional institutions in the modernization process, Samuel Huntington pointed out the dilemma faced by the "modernizing monarch" who

is the prisoner of the institution that makes this modernization possible. His policies require the expansion of political participation but his institution does not permit it. The success of modernization in the first stage depends upon strengthening the power of this traditional institution, whose legitimacy the process of modernization progressively undermines.[2]

The more the monarch modernizes the social and economic structure, the more exposed is the political institution which has made this possible. If a critical point has not yet been reached in Nepal, it is precisely because the programs of economic and social reform the royal regime has sought to introduce have never been implemented with any vigor and thus have had little direct impact upon the broad masses of the people. But again referring to the experiences of other countries, it is doubtful whether this consensus-by-apathy can be maintained indefinitely. It is only when the modernizing process King Mahendra has set into motion is further advanced that we

[1] On this question, see Fred R. von der Mehden, *Politics of Developing Nations* (Englewood Cliffs, N.J.: Prentice-Hall, 1964).

[2] Samuel Huntington, *Political Order in Changing Societies* (New Haven: Yale University Press, 1968), p. 168.

will know whether his priorities have been right, or whether his approach to modernization has any unique advantages over that proposed by the advocates of a political party system. For Nepal, situated precariously in the buffer area between competing political and ideological systems that intrude constantly upon the country's internal development, the choice may well prove to be a question of survival.

A Guide to the
Literature on Nepal

This guide is intended to serve as an introduction to the
literature on Nepal and to some of the academic institutions
with a primary research interest in this country. The older
(pre-1957) Western language works are listed in Dr. Margaret
W. Fisher's "Selected Bibliography of Source Materials for
Nepal" which can be obtained (without charge) from the
Institute of International Studies, University of California,
Berkeley. In this selection of readings, only Western language
works not cited in the above, and Asian language publications
(Nepali, unless otherwise indicated), have been included.

Libraries and Archives

The organization of libraries and archives in Nepal is still
in a formative stage, with a few important exceptions. The
magnificent Sanskrit, Nepali, and Newari language manuscript
resources at the Durbar (formerly Bir) Library in Kathmandu,
for instance, were organized and catalogued in the nineteenth
century and important additions to the collection continue to
be made. The Central Library in Kathmandu has a large number of Western and Nepali language publications on Nepal,
but the most comprehensive collection of post-1951 Nepali
publications is to be found at the Madan Trust Library in
Lalitpur, near Kathmandu.

A National Archives has recently been established in Nepal but it will be some time before it will become the principal depository for government documents. It is still necessary to utilize the archives of the various government departments, only a few of which are arranged on an organized basis. The National Archives of India in New Delhi and the India Office Library (IOL) in London also contain important archival resources for the pre-1947 period, in particular the reports, consultations, and correspondence of the British Government of India.

Library resources outside of Nepal are all somewhat unsatisfactory, but there are several important collections. The Indian School of International Studies Library in New Delhi has the best single collection in India on contemporary Nepal, including useful newspaper clipping files. For pre-1947 publications, the National Library in Calcutta is probably the most useful.

The School of Oriental and African Studies (SOAS) at the University of London has a reasonably good collection of Western and Asian language publications on Nepal, particularly in the field of anthropology. Of the relatively meager pre-1947 Nepali language publications, the IOL in London has what may be a complete collection. The IOL, Cambridge University Library, and the British Museum Library also have small but important collections of Nepali manuscripts in Sanskrit and the various languages of Nepal, including Newari and Kirati.

In Paris, the Centre d'Etudes Népalaises has a core library on contemporary Nepal, while the Istituto Italiano per il Medio ed Estremo Oriente in Rome has a limited but impressive collection of Nepali, Newari, and Sanskrit manuscripts. In the United States, the best single collection is at the Center for South Asia Studies Library at the University of California, Berkeley. The University of Pennsylvania Library and the Library of Congress also have limited collections of Nepali language publications.

Historical Studies

The first Nepali historian to publish a general history of Nepal that was more than a dynastic geneological account was Ambika Prasad Upadhyaya, *Nepal ko Itihas* (History of Nepal) (Banaras: Indian Press, 1929), 295 pp. The events leading up to the overthrow of the Rana regime in 1951 also stimulated interest in the history of the country. Probably the most influential publication of that period was the work of a Nepali scholar resident in India, Balchandra Sharma, *Nepal ko Aitihasik Ruprekha* (An Outline History of Nepal) (Banaras: Madhan Prasad Sharma, 1951), 440 pp. Since the revolution, historical research has developed to a remarkable extent and a number of Nepali scholars are now engaged in this task. The tendency has been to concentrate upon specific events or eras but several general histories based in part upon Nepali sources never utilized by Western scholars have also been published. Three of the more notable of these are Hemlall Joshi, *Nepal ko Itihas* (History of Nepal) (Kathmandu: Bhagavati Press, 1953), 98 pp.; Ishwar Raj Aryal, *Nepal ko Nayan Itihas* (New History of Nepal) (Banaras: Bhargav Bhukar Press, 1956), 255 pp.; and Dhundiraj Bhandari, *Nepal ko Aitihasik Vivechana* (Historical Analysis of Nepal) (Banaras: Krishna Kumari, 1958), 368 pp.

ANCIENT AND MEDIEVAL PERIODS

Since 1951, Nepali historians have made several major contributions to the literature on the ancient and medieval periods in Nepali history. Many of these are article length publications in such Nepali journals as *Sanskrit Sandesh, Purnima, Pragati,* and *Sharada.* A large number of inscriptions and selections from manuscripts have been published in such series as the *Itihas Prakas* (Lights on History), nine volumes published by the Itihas Prakas Mandal; *Aitihasik Patra Sangraha*

(A Collection of Historical Letters), several volumes published by the Nepal Samskritik Parishad; and *Ablilekh Sangraha* (Collection of Inscriptions), eleven volumes published by the Samshodhan Mandal. Somewhat different in character, but also based upon inscription and manuscript sources, are the numerous brief publications of the *Itihas Samshodhan* (Corrections of History), published by the Samshodhan Mandal. These are often controversial but useful corrections of alleged errors made by both Asian and Western scholars of Nepali history.

In addition to these sources a number of volumes on the medieval period in Nepali history have been published: Dilli Raman Regmi, *Ancient and Medieval Nepal* (Kathmandu: 1952), 178 pp., and *Medieval Nepal*, 3 volumes (Calcutta: Firma K. L. Mukhopadhyay, 1965–66); Surya Bikram Jñawali, *Nepal Upatyakako Madhya Kalin Itihas* (Medieval History of the Nepal Valley) (Kathmandu: Royal Nepal Academy, 1962), 338 pp.; Bhairab Bahadur Pradhan, *Madhya Kalin Nepal* (Medieval Nepal) (Kathmandu: Shivarani Press, 1954), 72 pp.; and Luciano Petech, *Mediaeval History of Nepal* (Roma: Istituto Italiano per il Medio ed Estremo Oriente, 1958), 238 pp. The first four of these studies are based on Nepali and Western sources, but Petech has also used Chinese and Tibetan sources extensively.

MODERN PERIOD

The modern period in Nepali history commences with the conquest of Nepal (Kathmandu) Valley by the Gorkha ruler, Prithvi Narayan Shah, in 1769–1770. A number of volumes on this period detail the background to this event which marks the genesis of the contemporary Nepali nation: *Gorkha Vamsavali* (Genealogy of the Gorkha Dynasty) (Banaras: Yoga Pracharini Association, n.d.), 144 pp.; Yogi Naraharinath, *Gorkhaliharu ko Sainik Itihas* (Military History of the

Gorkhas) (Kathmandu: Annapurna Press, 1954), 24 pp.; Yogi Naraharinath and Baburam Acharya, *Shri Panch Bada Maharaja Prithvi Narayan Shah ko Divya Upadesh* (The Divine Council of the Great Maharaja, Prithvi Narayan Shah) (Kathmandu: Shri Bagishwar Press, 1953), 38 pp.; Som Dhwaj Bisht, *Shahi Sainik Itihas* (History of the Shah Army) (Kathmandu: 1963); and Surya Bikram Jñawali, *Nepal Vijeta Shri Panch Prithvi Narayan Shah ko Jivani* (Life of King Prithvi Narayan Shah, Conqueror of Nepal) (Darjeeling: Nepali Sahitya Sammelan, 1935), 205 pp.

Contemporary Nepali historians have also published widely on the period between the conquest of Kathmandu Valley and the establishment of the Rana family regime (1770–1847). In addition to the general histories already cited, a number of publications should be mentioned: Baburam Acharya, "Bhimsen Thapa ko Patan" (The Downfall of Bhimsen Thapa), *Pragati*, II, No. 4 (1957), 115–123; Surya Bikram Jñawali, *Amar Singh Thapa* (Darjeeling: Ratnakar Press, 1951), 230 pp. (in Hindi); Chittaranjan Nepali, *Rana Bahadur Shah* (Kathmandu: Shrimati Mary Rajbhandari, 1964), 154 pp., and *Janaral Bhimsen Thapa ra Tatkalin Nepal* (General Bhimsen Thapa and the Nepal of His Day) (Kathmandu: Jorganesh Press, 1957), 334 pp.; and Dilli Raman Regmi, *Modern Nepal* (Calcutta: Firma K. L. Mukhopadhyay, 1961), 333 pp.

For some reason, the Rana era (1847–1951) has not as yet been the subject of intensive inquiry. There are several accounts by British officials who had some contact with Nepal in this period including *While Memory Serves* (London: Cassel, 1950), by the former British Commander in Chief in India, Sir Francis Tuker. There was also an outpouring of stridently anti-Rana publications by Nepali political exiles in India in the 1947–51 period, of which the best known was Dilli Raman Regmi's *A Century of Family Autocracy* (Banaras: Nepali National Congress, 1950). Several of the general histories already cited, particularly Balchandra Sharma and Dhundiraj Bhandari, have treated the Rana period at some length, but neither Nepali nor Western scholars have yet made full use of the massive quantities of documentary and manuscript resources available. The most thorough study so far, based primarily upon the records at the National Archives of India, is Satish Kumar, *Rana Polity in Nepal: Origin and Growth* (Bombay and New York: Asia Publishing House, 1967), 195 pp.

Social and Physical Environment

Sociological material is, of course, to be found in most of the histories and other serious accounts already listed. But probably the most valuable Nepali source on the social system of the various ethnic groups in Nepal are the several editions of the *Muluki Ain* (Legal Code) published between 1854 and 1963. The general practice of the Nepal government has been to accept local customs and practices, and to incorporate them in the legal code as long as they do not conflict with certain fundamental shastric Hindu principles. The various editions of the code, therefore, are an excellent source of information on the widely varied social systems in Nepal. If studied comparatively, they would also yield much useful data on the process of "Sanskritization." The latest legal code (1963) is readily available, but copies of the earlier editions are rare. English translations of the various editions by the Regmi Research Project in Kathmandu are well advanced.

Field work in the anthropology and sociology of Nepal became possible only after the overthrow of the Rana regime in 1951. Since then, particularly in the past decade, this has become the field of highest concentration among foreign scholars interested in Nepal, with a number of institutions in several countries making significant contributions.

The premier institution in this field, both in date of origin and in the quantity of field research undertaken, is the SOAS at the University of London where the Nepal program is under the directorship of Christoph von Fürer-Haimendorf. Among his many contributions are *The Sherpas of Nepal: Buddhist Highlanders* (Berkeley and Los Angeles: University of California Press, 1964), 298 pp.; "Unity and Diversity in the Chetri Caste of Nepal" and "Caste Concepts and Status Distinctions in Buddhist Communities of Western Nepal" in Fürer-Haimendorf, ed., *Caste and Kin in Nepal, India, and Ceylon: Anthropological Studies in Hindu-Buddhist Contact Zones* (Bombay: Asia Publishing House, 1966), pp. 11–64 and 140–160; and "Caste in the Multi-Ethnic Society of Nepal," *Contributions to Indian Sociology*, IV (April, 1960), 12–32. Another important study sponsored by the SOAS was that of Colin Rosser, "Social Mobility in the Newar Caste System," in Fürer-Haimendorf, ed., *op. cit.*, pp. 68–139.

The Centre d'Etudes Népalaises of the Centre National de la Recherches Scientifique in Paris, now under the directorship of Corneille Jest, has also sponsored several field research programs in various sections of Nepal by such scholars as A. W. MacDonald, Marc Gaborieau, Mireille Helffer, and Bernard Pignede. A study on the Gurung community in western Nepal by Pignede, *Les Gurung, une Population Himalayenne du Népal* (Paris: La Haye, Mouton, 1966), 303 pp., has been published as well as a number of monographs and articles on such castes and ethnic groups as the Gagñe, Thakalis, Tharus, and the Muslim community of Kathmandu valley. Two issues of the journal, *Objets et Monde* (Vol. VI [Summer, 1966] and Vol. IX [Spring, 1969]) consisted of contributions by members of the Center.

Several Japanese scholars have also made substantial contributions in the fields of anthropology and ecology. A group under the leadership of Jiro Kawakita accompanied the 1953 Japanese Himalayan expedition. Kawakita and Sasuki Nakao contributed Part I of a three volume study published in *The*

Japanese Journal of Ethnology, Vol. XIX, No. 1 (1955) under the title "Nepal: Some Ethno-geographical Observations in the Nepal Himalaya" (A summary English translation has been published). Another member of this group, Shigeru Iijima, published an article on the "Ecology, Economy, and Social System in the Nepal Himalayas," *Developing Economies,* II (March, 1964), 92–105.

The leading American anthropologist in Nepal studies is John T. Hitchcock, whose list of publications on Nepal includes *The Magars of Banyan Hill* (New York: Holt, Rinehart and Winston, 1966), 115 pp.; "Some Effects of Recent Change in Rural Nepal," *Human Organization,* XXII (Spring, 1963), 75–82; and "Sub-Tribes in the Magar Community in Nepal," *Asian Survey,* V (April, 1965), 207–215.

Anthropology is still in an early stage of development in Nepal when compared to other social sciences and history, but a number of younger scholars are coming to the fore. Two of the more important publications by Nepalis in the field are Dor Bahadur Bista, *The People of Nepal* (Kathmandu: Department of Publicity, 1967), 173 pp.; and Gopal Singh Nepali, *The Newars: An Ethno-Sociological Study of a Himalayan Community* (Bombay: United Asia Publications, 1965), 476 pp.

One of the earlier studies of the physical environment in the post-1951 period was that by Pradyumna P. Karan, *Nepal: A Physical and Cultural Geography* (Lexington: University of Kentucky Press, 1960), 100 pp. Toni Hagen, a Swiss geologist who spent approximately seven years in Nepal as a U.N. consultant to the Nepal government, traversed the entire country many times in the course of his work. His study, *Nepal: The Kingdom in the Himalayas,* tr. by Britta M. Charleston (Berne, Switzerland: Kummerly and Frey, 1961), U.S. distributor, Rand McNally, is the best single source on both the topography and geology of Nepal. Another useful study on this subject is S. H. Shrestha, *Modern Geography of Nepal* (Kathmandu: Vishwakarma Press, 1968), 164 pp.

The numerous accounts of the mountaineering expeditions that have launched their campaigns against the Himalayan peaks from the Nepal side of the range are also valuable sources of information on the areas of their operation. These are usually widely publicized and are readily available in most libraries, and we will not list them here. The Forschungs-unternehmen Nepal Himalaya of Munich, West Germany, under the directorship of Walter Hellmich, has concentrated its attention on scientific research in Nepal, the results of which are published in an annual volume, *Khumbu Himal*, published by the institute.

Government and Politics

The large number of government publications and private newspapers and journals in Nepal provide a rich source of basic data on the politics and administration of the country. Through the U.S. Public Law 480 Program, many of these documents and publications are made available to the various depository libraries in the United States. The Regmi Research Project in Kathmandu also sponsors a program under which translations of Nepali publications and government documents are made available to libraries and research institutions throughout the world. Included in these series are daily press reports, a weekly press digest, translations of the *Nepal Gazette* published by the Nepal government, and the Nepal Law Translation series.

There are several general surveys which have analyzed the political process and institutions in post-revolutionary Nepal: George L. Harris *et al.*, *U.S. Army Areas Handbook for Nepal (with Sikkim and Bhutan)* (Washington: Government Printing Office, 1964), 448 pp.; Leo E. Rose, *Nepal: Government and Politics* (New Haven: Human Relations Area Files, 1956), 360 pp.; Surendra B. Shrestha, *How Nepal is Governed* (Kathmandu: Pashupati Press, n.d. [Preface dated 1965]), 293 pp.; and Bhuwan Lal Joshi and Leo E. Rose, *Democratic Innova-*

tions in Nepal: A Case Study of Political Acculturation (Berkeley: University of California Press, 1966), 551 pp.

The evolution of constitutional law in Nepal and, more specifically, the 1959 and 1962 constitutions have been the subject of several studies: Ram Bahadur, *Nepal ko Samvidhan* (Constitution of Nepal) (Kathmandu: Chhatra Mitra Prakashan, 1962), 92 pp.; Narendra Goyal, *The King and His Constitution* (New Delhi: Nepal Trading Corporation, n.d.), 140 pp.; Laxman Bahadur Hamal, *Nepal ko Samvidhan* (Constitution of Nepal) (Biratnagar: Parvanchal Prakash, 1960), 78 pp.; Tirtha R. Tuladhar, *The Constitution of Nepal* (Kathmandu: HMG Press, 1966), 124 pp.; and Dundiraj Sharma, *Parliament ra Sallahakar Sabha* (Parliament and the Advisory Assembly) (Kathmandu: National Academy, 1959), 439 pp.

A large and growing body of literature on the panchayat system introduced in 1962 includes, in addition to the general political studies already cited, Pashupati Shamsher J.B.R. and Mohammad Mohsin, *A Study Report on the Pattern of Emerging Leadership in Panchayats* (Kathmandu: Panchayat Ministry, 1967), 45 pp.; *Pronouncements of King Mahendra (on Panchayatcracy)*, collected and translated by Daman R. Tuladhar (Kathmandu: HMG Press, 1968), 223 pp. (with Nepali and English texts); Leo E. Rose, "Nepal Experiments with 'Traditional' Democracy," *Pacific Affairs*, XXXVI (Spring, 1963), 16–31; Indra Prasad Kaphey, *Fundamental Basis of Panchayat Democratic System* (Kathmandu: Nepal Press, 1967), 239 pp.; and Tulsi Giri *et al.*, *Panchayat* (Kathmandu: Department of Publicity and Broadcasting, 1963), 74 pp. A major study of Panchayat institutions by Ishwar Baral is also scheduled for publication in 1970.

A number of detailed studies of the administrative system have been undertaken by foreign consultants connected either with the foreign aid programs, the Ford Foundation, or the United Nations specialized agencies. While none of these have been published for general circulation, several of them are available in typescript or mimeograph form in the more comprehensive library collections on Nepal. There is no exhaustive study of administrative institutions by Nepali scholars or government servants published as yet, but several useful articles or monographs are: Ramchand Malhotra, "Public Administration in Nepal," *Indian Journal of Public Administration,* IV (October–December, 1958), 451–464; Mangal K. Shrestha, *A Handbook of Public Administration in Nepal* (Kathmandu: Department of Publicity and Broadcasting, 1962), 121 pp.; *Anchal Ebam Vikas Zilla Vibhajan Samiti ko Report* (Report of the Development District and Zonal Demarcation Committee) (Kathmandu: HMG Press, 1962), 47 pp.; "Prashasan Shakti Vikendrikaren Ayog ko Prativedan" (Report of the Commission on Decentralization of Administrative Authority), *Gorkhapatra,* 18 July, 1964; Lok Raj Baral, "Zilla Prashasan ma Bada Hakim ko Sthan" (The Position of the Bada Hakim in District Administration), *Gorkhapatra,* 8 December, 1962, p. 10; and Ganga Vikram Sijapati, "Nepal Prashasan Vyovastha Vikash ko Ruprekha" (Outline of the Evolution of the Administrative System in Nepal), *Nepali,* No. 13 (November, 1962–January, 1963), pp. 25–56.

POLITICAL PARTIES

A large quantity of ephemeral political party material appeared between 1951 and 1961, including party constitutions, manifestoes, policy statements, organizational histories, and summary accounts of party meetings. Most of them are no longer available in the Kathmandu libraries, but some can be found in the libraries in India and the United States mentioned above. During the period of their legality, most of the political parties published newspapers or periodicals, which were the best sources of information on these organizations. Some of the more influential were *Mashal* (Communist Party),

Navayug (Communist Party), *Nepal Pukar* (Nepali Congress), *Rashtravani* (Gorkha Parishad), and *Samyukta Prayas* (National Democratic Party). Since 1961, parties have been banned and there is, therefore, no party press as such. The *Nepal Today* (Calcutta), however, is published by the Nepali Congress Party-in-Exile, while the *Samiksha* (Kathmandu) reportedly reflects the views of one wing of the Nepal Communist Party.

The best single study of the parties in the 1951–1961 period is Anirudha Gupta's *Politics in Nepal: A Study of Post-Rana Political Developments and Party Politics* (Bombay: Allied Publishers, 1964), 332 pp. For a dramatic account of the personalities and organizations that led the revolutionary movement against the Rana regime, see Bhola Chatterji, *A Study of Recent Nepalese Politics* (Calcutta: The World Press, 1967), 190 pp. There have been no studies as yet on such topics as parties and party politics by Nepali scholars, but there are several publications which present intimate insights into the functioning and character of these organizations. Two of the most detailed are Grishma Bahadur Devkota, *Nepal ko Rajnaitik Darpan* (A Political Mirror of Nepal) (Kathmandu: K. C. Gautam, 1959), 766 pp.; and Dharma Ratna "Yami," *Nepal ko Kura* (Facts about Nepal) (Kathmandu: 1956).

Information on the operation of illegal Nepali political organizations after 1961 is still relatively difficult to find. See the Joshi and Rose volume cited above, and Leo E. Rose, "Communism under High Atmospheric Conditions: The Party in Nepal" in Robert A. Scalapino, ed., *The Communist Revolution in Asia* (New York: Prentice-Hall, 1965), pp. 243–272. A collection of pamphlet publications by the Nepali Communist Party-in-Exile in India between 1961 and 1969 is available in the South Asia Center library at the University of California, Berkeley.

INTERNATIONAL RELATIONS

Nepal's critical geopolitical situation has naturally directed attention to the state's relations with its foreign neighbors. There are numerous papers, articles, and pamphlets on this subject, but some of the more useful have been: Jagdish Prasad Sharma, "Nepal's Foreign Policy, 1947–1962," Ph.D. dissertation, University of Pennsylvania, 1968, 318 pp.; Rishikesh Shaha, *Nepal and the World,* 2nd ed. (Kathmandu: Nepali Congress, 1955), 54 pp.; Bishwa Pradhan, *Foreign Policy and Diplomacy* (Delhi: Rakesh Press, 1964), 96 pp.; and *Statement of Principles: Major Foreign Speeches by His Majesty, King Mahendra,* 2 volumes (Kathmandu: Department of Publicity and Broadcasting, 1962 and 1964), 39 and 44 pp.

Texts of treaties between Nepal and British India and Tibet can be found in C. U. Aitchison, *A Collection of Treaties, Engagements, and Sanads Relating to India and Neighbouring Countries,* Vol. XIV (New Delhi: Central Publishing Branch, 1929). For the Nepali texts of these and other treaties, see Yogi Naraharinath, *Itihas Prakash ma Sandhi Patra Sangraha* (A Collection of Treaties in the Light of History) (Kathmandu: 1966), 784 pp. A comprehensive selection of treaties and related documents for the post-1947 period by A. H. Bahsin is scheduled for publication in 1970.

Two studies of Nepal's relations with British India have been based primarily upon the resources at the National Archives of India in New Delhi: K. C. Chaudhuri, *Anglo-Nepalese Relations, from the Earliest Times of the British Rule in India till the Gurkha War* (Calcutta: Modern Book Agency, 1960), 181 pp.; and Bhairava Datt Sanwal, *Nepal and the East India Company* (Bombay: Asia Publishing House, 1965), 345 pp. Among the large number of official Nepali publications on contemporary Nepal-India relations, two of the more useful are Yadunath Khanal, *Reflections on Nepal-India Rela-*

tions (collection of speeches by the author while Ambassador to India) (Delhi: Rakesh Press, 1964), 98 pp; and Jitendra Raj Sharma, *Nepal-India Relations* (Kathmandu: Department of Publicity and Broadcasting, 1963), 40 pp.

Nepal's strategic situation between India and China, and the problems this has raised in the state's relations with both powers, have been the subjects of several studies: Girilal Jain, *India Meets China in Nepal* (Bombay and New York: Asia Publishing House, 1959), 177 pp.; Leo E. Rose, "Sino-Indian Rivalry and the Himalayan Border States," *Orbis*, V (July, 1961), 198–215; Margaret W. Fisher and Joan V. Bondurant, *Indian Views of Sino-Indian Relations*, Indian Press Digests Project Monograph No. 1 (Berkeley: University of California Press, 1956), 163 pp.; Satish Kumar, "Chinese Aggression and Indo-Nepalese Relations," *United Asia*, XV (November, 1963), 740–744; Prakash Bahadur, *Hostile Expeditions and International Law* (Kathmandu: Department of Publicity and Broadcasting, 1962), 62 pp.; and Poorna Bahadur, M.A., *Nepal behind the Screen* (Kathmandu: Nepal Youth League, 1957), 55 pp.

Nepal's relations with Tibet and China have also been a subject of growing interest to both Nepali and foreign scholars. For the pre-1950 period, see Baburam Acharya, *Chin ra Tibet sita Nepal ko Sambandha* (Nepal's Relations with China and Tibet) (Kathmandu: Jorganesh Press, 1958), 35 pp.; "Historicus" (Rishikesh Shaha), "Nepal-China Relations," *The Nepal Guardian*, No. 2 (June, 1954), pp. 37–47; Bishnu Prasad Poudel, "Nepal's Relations with Tibet, 1792–1856," Ph.D. dissertation, Indian School of International Studies, 1963, 264 MS pp.; Nakamasa Suzuki, *China, Tibet, and India: Their Early International Relations* (Tokyo: Hitotsubashi Shobo, 1962) (in Japanese); *Chin-Ting K'uo-erh-k'a Chi-Lueh* (Official Summary Account of the Pacification of the Gurkhas) (Peking: 1796); and Mayura Jang Kunwar (Brown), "China

and War in the Himalayas, 1792–1793," *The English Historical Review,* LXXVII (April, 1962), 283–297.

For relations between China and Nepal since the resumption of diplomatic relations between the two powers in 1955,
see Chinese People's Institute of Foreign Affairs, *New Development in Friendly Relations Between China and Nepal* (Peking: Foreign Language Press, 1960), 92 pp.; Tirtha R. Tuladhar, *Nepal-China, A Story of Friendship* (Kathmandu:
Department of Publicity and Broadcasting, n.d.), 47 pp.;
Satish Kumar, "Nepal and China," *Indian Journal of Political
Science,* XXIV (January–March, 1963), 79–93; Huang Sheng-
chang, "China and Nepal," *People's China* (May 1, 1956), pp.
8–10; and Roger Dial, "Flexibility in Chinese Foreign Relations: Nepal, a Case Study," M.A. thesis, University of California, Berkeley, 1967. 249 pp. A study by Leo E. Rose of
Nepal's role in Himalayan area politics and its relations with
China, Tibet, and India will be published in 1970 by the
University of California Press.

ECONOMIC POLICY

Basic data on the program for the modernization of the
Nepali economy are found in the various reports of such government offices as the Bureau of Statistics, the National Planning Council, the Ministry of Economic Planning, the Ministry of Finance, and the Ministry of Land Reform. While the
three plans (two 5-year and one 3-year) which have set the
goals of the government's economic development program have
never been published in their entirety, summary accounts of
these documents have been issued by the National Planning
Council. Economic legislation and ordinances are published
in the *Nepal Gazette,* and translations of these are available
through the Regmi Research Project in Kathmandu.

The literature on economic development in Nepal is still
very limited, but there are a number of pioneer publications

by Nepali economists: Yadav Prasad Pant, *Economic Development of Nepal* (Allahabad: Kitab Mahal, 1965), 116 pp.; Badri Prasad Shrestha, *The Economy of Nepal or a Study in Problems and Processes of Industrialization* (Bombay: Vora, 1967), 274 pp., and *Monetary Policy in an Emerging Economy: A Case Study of Nepal* (Kathmandu: Ratna Pustak Bhandar, 1965), 117 pp.; Mahesh C. Regmi, *Land Tenure and Taxation in Nepal*, 4 volumes (Berkeley: Institute of International Studies, University of California, 1963–1968); and Jagdish Chandra Ojha and Ram Prasad Rajbahak, *Banking and Modern Currency in Nepal*, 2nd ed. (Kathmandu: Educational Enterprise, 1965), 173 pp.

The comparatively massive input of foreign economic assistance into Nepal has resulted in an equally large volume of reports on the country's economic development problems. Some of these, and particularly those of the American and Israeli aid programs, are available in mimeograph form in various library collections. The published literature on the role of foreign aid in Nepal is still very limited, but there are two publications which should be mentioned. The first is by the Nepali economist Yadav Prasad Pant, *Nepal's Economic Development on International Basis: An Analysis of Foreign Aid Utilization* (Kathmandu: Educational Enterprise, 1962), 87 pp. The second publication is by an American political scientist, one of whose themes was the impact of foreign aid programs on the government and politics of Nepal: Eugene B. Mihaly, *Foreign Aid and Politics in Nepal: A Case Study* (New York: Oxford University Press, 1965), 202 pp.

Suggestions for Further Reading

For the student who wishes to extend his knowledge of Nepal, the following English language publications have been selected as the most pertinent.

Bista, Dor Bahadur. *The People of Nepal*. Kathmandu: Department of Publicity, 1967.

Fürer-Haimendorf, Christoph von. "Caste in the Multi-Ethnic Society of Nepal," *Contributions to Indian Sociology*, IV (April, 1960), 12–32.

——. *The Sherpas of Nepal: Buddhist Highlanders*. Berkeley and Los Angeles: University of California Press, 1964.

——, ed. *Caste and Kin in Nepal, India, and Ceylon: Anthropological Studies in Hindu-Buddhist Contact Zones*. Bombay: Asia Publishing House, 1966.

Gupta, Anirudha. *Politics in Nepal: A Study of Post-Rana Political Developments and Party Politics*. Bombay: Allied Publishers, 1964.

Hagen, Toni. *Nepal: The Kingdom in the Himalayas*. Tr. by Britta M. Charleston. Berne, Switzerland: Kummerly and Frey, 1961.

Harris, George L., *et al. U.S. Army Areas Handbook for Nepal (with Sikkim and Bhutan)*. Washington: Government Printing Office, 1964.

Hitchcock, John T. *The Magars of Banyan Hill*. New York: Holt, Rinehart and Winston, 1966.

Joshi, Bhuwan Lal, and Leo E. Rose. *Democratic Innovations in Nepal: A Case Study of Political Acculturation*. Berkeley and Los Angeles: University of California Press, 1966.

Karan, Pradyumna P. *Nepal: A Physical and Cultural Geography*. Lexington: University of Kentucky Press, 1960.

Mihaly, Eugene Bramer. *Foreign Aid and Politics in Nepal: A Case Study*. New York: Oxford University Press, 1965.

Regmi, Dilli Raman. *Modern Nepal*. Calcutta: Firma K. L. Mukhopadhyay, 1961.

Regmi, Mahesh Chandra. *Land Tenure and Taxation in Nepal*. 4 volumes. Berkeley: Institute of International Studies, University of California, 1963–1968.

Rose, Leo E. "Nepal Experiments with 'Traditional' Democracy," *Pacific Affairs*, XXXVI (Spring, 1963), 16–31.

——. "Communism under High Atmospheric Conditions: The Party in Nepal," in Robert A. Scalapino, ed., *The Communist Revolution in Asia*. New York: Prentice-Hall, 1969. Pp. 363–390.

Rosser, Colin. "Social Mobility in the Newar Caste System," in Fürer-Haimendorf, ed., *Caste and Kin in Nepal, India, and Ceylon*, pp. 68–139.

Shrestha, Badri Prasad. *The Economy of Nepal, or a Study in Problems and Processes of Industrialization*. Bombay: Vora, 1967.

Index

Acharya, Tanka Prasad, 29, 53, 67, 169
Adhikari, Manmohan, 113
Administrative institutions, 63–79, 170; tour commissions, 60, 76; Central Secretariat, 65–72; Public Service Commission, 66–67; Palace Secretariat, 72–74; regional administration, 74–79; local administration, 79–83
Agrarian policy, 122–129
Amatya, Tulsi Lal, 111, 112
Arya Samaj, 93–94

Birta abolition, 124
Borders, Nepali, 4, 5
Brahmans, 10, 92
Britain, relations with Nepal, 16–18, 145, 147–148

Central Secretariat, 65–72
Chautarias, 19
Chettri, 10
China, relations with Nepal, 16–17, 136–137, 140, 142, 146, 149–150, 152–156, 159
Class and professional organizations, 57, 116–119
Constitutional system: 1948 Constitution, 26, 46–48, 85–86; 1951 government act, 39, 48–50, 166; 1959 Constitution, 30–31, 32, 50–51; 1962 Constitution, 40–41, 51–56

District panchayats, 78

Ex-Servicemen's Association, 116

Foreign aid, 140–143
Foreign policy, 144–163; see also International relations

Gandak River, 5
Gorkha, 15, 16
Gorkha Parishad, 31, 100
Governmental system, see Administrative institutions, Constitutional system, Judicial institutions, Panchayat system, Political system, and Rana family regime
Gurkha recruitment, 147–148
Gurungs, 12

Himalayas, 6–8; passes, 4; inner valleys, 8
Hinduism, 10–14, 34–35

India, relations with Nepal, 26–27, 96, 100, 135, 138–139, 140, 150–152, 156–162
Industrial policy, 129–134
Inner Terai, 6, 7
International relations: with Tibet, 1, 16–17, 134–135, 136–137; with Sikkim, 4, 17; with Britain, 16–18, 145, 147–148; with China, 16–17, 136–137, 140, 142, 146, 149–150, 152–156, 159; with India,

International relations (*continued*)
26–27, 96, 100, 135, 138–139, 140,
150–152, 156–162; with U.S.S.R.,
133, 142, 149, 153, 160; with
Pakistan, 137; with U.S. 142, 149

Jana Congress, 101
Judicial institutions, 83–91; court
system, 84–88; Bharadari Court,
84; Supreme Court, 85–88; law
system, 88–91; Muluki Ain, 88–
90, 91

Kali River, 5
Karnali River, 5
Kerong Pass, 2
Kisan Sangh, 116
Koirala, Bishweshwar Prasad, 27,
28, 31, 95, 101, 154–157, 168
Koirala, Matrika Prasad, 27–29, 39,
101–102, 168
Koshi River, 5
Kshatriyas, 10, 19, 92–93
Kuti-Kodari Pass, 4

Land tenure, 125–128
Limbus, 12
Local administration, 79–83
Local (village and town) pan-
chayats, 79–83

Magars, 12
Mahabharat Range, 6, 7
Mishra, Bhadrakali, 101
Monarchy, 34–45, 55–56, 91; *see also*
Shah dynasty
Mount Everest (Sagarmatha), 8, 155

National Guidance Ministry, 58–59
National Panchayat, 54–57
Nepal Communist Party, 97, 103,
105, 108, 111–114, 116
Nepal Karmavir Mahamandal, 115
Nepal Praja Panchayat, 97
Nepali Congress: 1950 Revolution,
26–27, 97–98; cabinets, 27, 28, 31,

51, 75, 81, 99, 106–107, 168; or-
ganizations and policies, 67, 96,
102, 104–110, 140
Nepali Congress Progressive Group,
101
Nepali Democratic Congress, 96
Nepali Nagrik Adhikar Samiti, 94
Nepali National Congress, 95, 97
Newars, 11, 92–93

Pakistan, relations with Nepal, 137
Palace Secretariat, 72–74
Panchayat system, 32, 42, 52–62;
National Panchayat, 54–57; class
and professional organizations,
57, 116–119; national guidance,
58–59; district panchayats, 78;
local panchayats, 79–83
Pande family, 19
Plans and planning, 139–143
Political organizations, 56, 92–119
Political system: elections, 31; rep-
resentative institutions, 47, 48–
49, 54–57; Raj Sabha, 59–60
Prachand Gorkha, 94
Praja Parishad, 29–30, 67, 94–95
Public Service Commission, 66–67

Raj Sabha, 59–60
Raksha Dal, 98
Rana, Jang Bahadur, 20–21, 22, 45,
147
Rana family regime, 20, 21–22, 23,
25, 26, 36, 37; 1856 Sanad, 21–
22, 36, 38, 84–85; succession sys-
tem, 22–25
Rashtriya Praja Party, 101
Rayamajhi, Keshar Jang, 111
Regional administration (districts
and zones), 74–79
Regmi, D. R., 97
Representative institutions, 47, 48–
49, 54–57

Shah, King Mahendra B.B.: and
politics, 29, 30, 31, 32, 40–45, 50,

Shah, King Mahendra B.B. (*cont.*)
170–175; and administration, 66,
73–74; and political parties, 103,
104–114; and foreign policy, 151–
163
Shah, King Prithvi Narayan, 15–
16, 18, 144–145, 172
Shah, King Rajendra B.B., 20, 36
Shah, King Rana Bahadur, 35
Shah, King Surendra B.B., 21, 36
Shah, King Tribhuvan B.B., 26–29,
38–39, 44, 49–50, 66, 72, 98
Shah dynasty, 15, 18, 19–20, 34–35,
60–61
Shamsher, Bharat, 110
Shamsher, Bhim, 24
Shamsher, Bir, 23, 147
Shamsher, Chandra, 23, 45
Shamsher, Mohan, 26, 27, 46, 99,
101
Shamsher, Padma, 26, 46
Shamsher, Subarna, 102
Shanti Raksha Swayam Sevak Ken-
dra, 116
Sharma, Balchandra, 101
Sherpas, 12–13

Shrestha, Pushpa Lal, 111, 112
Sikkim, relations with Nepal, 4, 17
Singh, Ganeshman, 102
Singh, K. I., 30, 98
Singh, Ranuddip, 22
Siwalik Mountains, 6, 7

Tamangs, 12
Terai, 6, 7
Thakalis, 13
Thakuri, 10
Thapa family, 10
Tharus, 11
Tibet, relations with Nepal, 1, 16–
17, 134–137
Tour commissions, 60, 76
Trade, foreign, 134–139
Trade routes, 2–4

United Democratic Party, 30
Upadhyaya, Shailendra Kumar, 111
Upadhyaya, Surya Prasad, 102
U.S., relations with Nepal, 142, 149
U.S.S.R., relations with Nepal, 133,
142, 149, 153, 160

UNIVERSITY LIBRARY
NOTTINGHAM

The Politics of Nepal

Persistence and Change in
an Asian Monarchy

Designed by R. E. Rosenbaum.
Composed by Vail-Ballou Press, Inc.,
in 11 point linotype Baskerville, 2 points leaded,
with display lines in Palatino.
Printed from letterpress plates by Vail-Ballou Press
on Warren's No. 66 Text, 60 pound basis,
with the Cornell University Press watermark.
Bound by Vail-Ballou Press
in Interlaken ALP book cloth
and stamped in All Purpose foil.